The Holy Word for Morning Revival

Taking the Shepherding Way to Preach the Gospel and Revive the Church

Witness Lee

Living Stream Ministry
Anaheim, CA • www.lsm.org

First Edition, April 2006.

ISBN 0-7363-3155-7

Published by

Living Stream Ministry
2431 W. La Palma Ave., Anaheim, CA 92801 U.S.A.
P. O. Box 2121, Anaheim, CA 92814 U.S.A.

Printed in the United States of America

06 07 08 09 10 11 12 / 10 9 8 7 6 5 4 3 2 1

Contents

Preface

1. This book is intended as an aid to believers in developing a daily time of morning revival with the Lord in His word. At the same time, it provides a partial review of the International Training for Elders and Responsible Ones held in Anaheim, California, March 31—April 2, 2006. Through intimate contact with the Lord in His word, the believers can be constituted with life and truth and thereby equipped to prophesy in the meetings of the church unto the building up of the Body of Christ.
2. The entire content of this book is taken primarily from the published training outlines, the text and footnotes of the Recovery Version of the Bible, selections from the writings of Witness Lee and Watchman Nee, and *Hymns,* all of which are published by Living Stream Ministry.
3. The book is divided into weeks. One training message is covered per week. Each week presents first the message outline, followed by six daily portions, a hymn, and then some space for writing. The message outline has been divided into days, corresponding to the six daily portions. Each daily portion covers certain points and begins with a section entitled "Morning Nourishment." This section contains selected verses and a short reading that can provide rich spiritual nourishment through intimate fellowship with the Lord. The "Morning Nourishment" is followed by a section entitled "Today's Reading," a longer portion of ministry related to the day's main points. Each day's portion concludes with a short list of references for further reading and some space for the saints to make notes concerning their spiritual inspiration, enlightenment, and enjoyment to serve as a reminder of what they have received of the Lord that day.
4. The space provided at the end of each week is for composing a short prophecy. This prophecy can be composed by considering all of our daily notes, the "harvest" of our inspirations during the week, and preparing a main point

with some sub-points to be spoken in the church meetings for the organic building up of the Body of Christ.

5. Following the last week in this volume, we have provided reading schedules for both the Old and New Testaments in the Recovery Version with footnotes. These schedules are arranged so that one can read through both the Old and New Testaments of the Recovery Version with footnotes in two years.
6. As a practical aid to the saints' feeding on the Word throughout the day, we have provided verse cards at the end of the volume, which correspond to each day's scripture reading. These may be cut out and carried along as a source of spiritual enlightenment and nourishment in the saints' daily lives.
7. The training message outlines were compiled by Living Stream Ministry from the writings of Witness Lee and Watchman Nee. The outlines, footnotes, and references in the Recovery Version of the Bible are by Witness Lee. All of the other references cited in this publication are from the published ministry of Witness Lee and Watchman Nee.

International Training for Elders and Responsible Ones

(Spring 2006)

General Subject:

Taking the Shepherding Way to Preach the Gospel and Revive the Church

Living a Shepherding Life for the Building Up of the Church

Scripture Reading: Luke 22:31-33; Mark 16:7; John 21:15-19; 2 Cor. 7:2-7; 12:15

Day 1 & Day 2

I. John 21, a chapter on shepherding, is the completion and consummation of the Gospel of John; shepherding is the key to the Gospel of John:

A. If we do not know what shepherding is, the entire Gospel of John will be in vain to us; it is only when we shepherd others that we can know John in an intrinsic way (3:16; 4:10, 14; 10:9-18; 21:15-17).

B. The Gospel of John is a book on Christ coming to be our life by cherishing and nourishing us; to cherish people is to make them happy, pleasant, and comfortable (Matt. 9:10; Luke 7:34), and to nourish people is to feed them with the all-inclusive Christ (Matt. 24:45-47):

1. When Christ as the God-Savior was recognized by Nathanael as the Son of God, He told him that he would see heaven opened and the angels of God ascending and descending on Him as the Son of Man, like the heavenly ladder seen by Jacob in his dream; this was a kind of cherishing to encourage Nathanael to follow Him so that he might participate in His nourishment with all the divine benefits as revealed in the entire Gospel of John (1:45-51).

2. When Christ as the God-Savior wanted to save an immoral woman of Samaria, He had to travel from Judea to Galilee through Samaria and detoured from the main way of Samaria to the city of Sychar, and He waited at the well of Jacob, near Sychar, for His object to come so that He might cherish

her by asking her to give Him something to drink and so that He might nourish her with the water of life, which is the flowing of the Triune God Himself (4:3-14).

3. When none of the accusing Pharisees could condemn the adulterous woman, Christ as the God-Savior, in His humanity, said to her, "Neither do I condemn you," to cherish her that He, as the great I Am, might nourish her with the freedom from sin and enable her to "sin no more" (8:3-11, 24, 34-36).

Day 3

II. After His resurrection, the Lord shepherded Peter and commissioned him to feed His lambs and shepherd His sheep; this is to incorporate the apostolic ministry with Christ's heavenly ministry to take care of God's flock, the church, which issues in the Body of Christ (21:15-17):

A. Peter was self-confident in his natural strength and ability, even to the point of thinking that he would follow the Lord both to prison and to death (Luke 22:33).

B. Peter was tested and he denied the Lord three times, even before a little maid (John 18:15-18, 25-27).

C. Peter was absolutely defeated and became a complete failure so that he might realize that he was absolutely untrustworthy and should no longer have any confidence in himself (Matt. 26:69-75; cf. Phil. 3:3).

D. The trials through which we pass are used by the Lord to sift and destroy our natural disposition and habits and bring in the constitution of the Holy Spirit in maturity and sweetness (Rom. 8:28; Luke 22:31-32; cf. Jer. 48:11).

E. The angel's message to the three sisters who discovered the resurrection of the Slave-Savior was for them to "go, tell His disciples and Peter" (Mark 16:7; cf. 1 Pet. 5:13):

1. The phrase *and Peter* indicates that although Peter failed, stumbled, and fell, the Lord had not forsaken him; *and Peter* also means *and you*—you who have failed like Peter.
2. May we all see what kind of heart the Lord has toward us; it is impossible for Him not to love you, for Him to forget you, or for Him to forsake you (Rom. 5:6-10; Zech. 2:8; Isa. 49:15-16).

F. The Lord came to restore Peter's love toward Him, to charge him with the shepherding of His church, and to prepare him for his martyrdom so that he would not follow Him with any confidence in his natural strength (John 21:15-19).

G. To bear fruit and feed others, we need to enjoy and flow out the riches of the divine life; this requires that we love Him (vv. 15-17; 7:38).

H. Through Peter's failure, he learned to serve the brothers by faith in the Lord and with humility, shepherding the flock of God (Luke 22:31-32; 1 Pet. 5:2-6).

Day 4 **III. Taking the shepherding way to preach the gospel and revive the church is a life of ministering Christ to others in love for the building up of the church; this life is a fruitful life (Acts 20:20, 31; 1 Cor. 8:1b; John 15:5):**

Day 5 A. In taking care of the churches and in shepherding the saints, what is needed is the intimate concern of a ministering life (2 Cor. 7:2-7; 12:15; Philem. 7, 12):

1. In shepherding the saints, it is possible that we may kill others; the reason for this killing, this fruitlessness, is the lack of intimate concern (cf. 2 Cor. 3:6):
   a. The milk of the word of God, the life supply of Christ, should be used to nourish the new believers in Christ, not to "boil" them (1 Pet. 2:2; Exo. 23:19b).

b. If we have the ability to carry on a work but lack an intimate concern, our work will be fruitless; our heart must be enlarged to embrace all believers regardless of their condition (2 Cor. 6:10-11).

2. How fruitful we are, how much fruit we bear, does not depend on what we are able to do; it depends on whether we have an intimate concern.
3. A ministering life is a life that warms up others; if we would minister life to the saints, we must have a genuine concern for them, a concern that is emotional, deep, and intimate.

Day 6

B. Love is the most excellent way for us to be anything and to do anything for the building up of the Body of Christ (2 Tim. 1:7; 1 Cor. 12:31b; 13:4-8, 13):

1. We must have the kind of love to go and tell the dormant ones who think that the church condemns them that the church does not condemn anyone; rather, the church wants to see all the dormant ones come back.
2. Without the Lord's mercy we would be the same as the dormant ones; therefore, we must love them.
3. It all depends upon love, as the wise king Solomon said, "Love covers all transgressions" (Prov. 10:12b).
4. "Knowledge puffs up, but love builds up" (1 Cor. 8:1b).

Morning Nourishment

John 21:15-17 **Then when they had eaten breakfast, Jesus said to Simon Peter, Simon, *son* of John, do you love Me more than these? He said to Him, Yes, Lord, You know that I love You. He said to him, Feed My lambs. He said to him again a second time, Simon, *son* of John, do you love Me? He said to Him, Yes, Lord, You know that I love You. He said to him, Shepherd My sheep. He said to him the third time, Simon, *son* of John, do you love Me? Peter was grieved that He said to him the third time, Do you love Me? And he said to Him, Lord, You know all things; You know that I love You. Jesus said to him, Feed My sheep.**

John 21 is a chapter on shepherding. In our crystallization-study of the Gospel of John we saw that this chapter is not merely an appendix but also the completion and consummation of the Gospel of John, a book on Christ being God coming to be our life. The writer of this Gospel spent twenty chapters to unveil such a Christ. Eventually, such a book has a conclusion on shepherding. If we do not know what shepherding is, the entire Gospel of John will be in vain to us. It is only when we shepherd others that we can know John in an intrinsic way. Shepherding is the key to the Gospel of John.

John 21:15 says, "Jesus said to Simon Peter, Simon, son of John, do you love Me more than these? He said to Him, Yes, Lord, You know that I love You." Peter said, "Lord, You know," because he had denied the Lord three times. He lost his natural confidence in his love toward the Lord. In restoring Peter's love toward Him, the Lord charged him to shepherd and feed His sheep.

Without shepherding, there is no way for us to minister life to others. John is the Gospel of life. If we want to enjoy life and minister life to others, we must shepherd them. The real ministering of life is shepherding by visiting and contacting people. (*The Vital Groups,* pp. 60-61)

Today's Reading

When we visit people, invite them to our home, or contact them before and after the meetings, we must be one with Christ to cherish and nourish them.

To cherish people is to make them happy and to make them feel pleasant and comfortable. We must have a pleasant countenance when we contact people....We must give people the impression that we are genuinely happy and pleasant. Otherwise, we will not be able to cherish them, to make them happy.

Then we should go on to nourish them. We do not nourish people when we speak to them about marriage, courtship, politics, the world situation, or education. To nourish people is to feed them with the all-inclusive Christ in His full ministry in three stages. When we speak to people about Christ, we should not speak to them in an incomprehensible way in a kind of language which they do not understand. We have to find a way to present the all-inclusive Christ to everyone.

In order to nourish people with Christ, we first have to seek Christ, experience Christ, gain Christ, enjoy Christ, and participate in Christ. In Philippians, especially in chapters two and three, Paul used different expressions and utterances to portray how he was seeking and pursuing Christ in order to gain Christ. He told us that we should do all things without murmurings and reasonings. The sisters who are seeking Christ should learn not to murmur, and the brothers should learn not to reason. If you murmur and reason, you will offend the indwelling Christ, who is the embodiment of the Triune God, because this God is working in you that you may work out your salvation (2:12-14). Our salvation is our gaining and experiencing Christ. To gain Christ is to work out our own daily organic salvation. (*The Vital Groups,* pp. 102-103)

Further Reading: The Vital Groups, msgs. 7, 11

Enlightenment and inspiration: ____________________

____

____

____

Morning Nourishment

Matt. 9:10 And as He was reclining *at table* in the house, behold, many tax collectors and sinners came and reclined together with Jesus and His disciples.

Luke 7:34 The Son of Man has come eating and drinking, and you say, Behold, a gluttonous man and a drunkard, a friend of tax collectors and sinners.

Matt. 24:45 Who then is the faithful and prudent slave, whom the master has set over his household to give them food at the proper time?

When Christ as the God-Savior was recognized by Nathanael as the Son of God, He answered him that he would see heaven opened and the angels of God ascending and descending on Him as the Son of Man, like the heavenly ladder seen by Jacob in his dream, as a kind of cherishing to encourage Nathanael to follow Him that he might participate in His nourishment with all the divine benefits as revealed in the entire Gospel of John (1:45-51).

When Christ as the God-Savior wanted to save an immoral woman of Samaria, He had to travel from Judea to Galilee through Samaria and detoured from the main way of Samaria to the city of Sychar, and He waited at the well of Jacob, near Sychar, for His object to come that He might cherish her by asking her to give Him something to drink so that He might nourish her with the water of life, which is the flowing Triune God Himself (4:1-14).

When none of the accusing Pharisees could condemn the adulterous woman, Christ as the God-Savior, in His humanity, said to her, "Neither do I condemn you," to cherish her that He, as the great I Am, might nourish her with the freedom from sin and enable her to "sin no more" (8:3-11, 24, 34-36). (*The Vital Groups,* pp. 99-100)

Today's Reading

The model of Jesus as the Son of Man cherishing people

needs to be reproduced in us so that we also will cherish others in His humanity.

To cherish people is to make them happy, to comfort them, to make them feel that you are pleasant to them, easy to be contacted in everything and in every way. Our contact with people must be so genuine. Genuineness can be produced only by the cross plus resurrection. Only a crossed-out, resurrected person can be genuine in everything.

Some people are charming, attractive, and cherishing in their natural humanity by birth. When such a person walks into a room, the atmosphere changes. A charming person must be very warm, not cold. Those who are charming in their natural humanity, however, are not real. Actually, they are performers, like actors in a theater. When you get close to a charming man, you will find out that he actually is not that charming. He was born with a mask. When the mask is taken away, he is different. To cherish people in our natural humanity is not genuine. This is why we must cherish people in the humanity of Jesus. The Lord's charming and cherishing are not natural but are by His resurrection life in humanity.

We should cherish people, not by our natural man, but by our regenerated man that has been conformed to the death of Christ. We have two men within us. Ephesians 4:22-24 reveals that we must put off the old man and put on the new man by being renewed in the spirit of our mind. The mingled spirit must invade, take over, occupy, and saturate our mind with divinity; then our mind becomes a renewed mind. Romans 12:2 says that we are to be transformed by the renewing of our mind. That renewing is to put off the old man and put on the new man. We must be a new man living not by our natural man but by our regenerated man with God Himself. (*The Vital Groups,* pp. 92, 97, 93, 97)

Further Reading: The Vital Groups, msg. 10

Enlightenment and inspiration: ______________

____

____

____

Morning Nourishment

John 21:17 He said to him the third time, Simon, *son* of John, do you love Me? Peter was grieved that He said to him the third time, Do you love Me? And he said to Him, Lord, You know all things; You know that I love You. Jesus said to him, Feed My sheep.

The Lord's shepherding was firstly in His earthly ministry (Matt. 9:36). The Lord saw the Israelites as sheep harassed by their leaders; they were cast away like sheep not having a shepherd. The Lord as the Shepherd of God's elect prayed, and God told His sent One to appoint twelve apostles that they might take care of the sheep of God (Matt. 10:1-6).

The Lord's shepherding is secondly in His heavenly ministry (1 Pet. 5:4) to take care of the church of God, issuing in His Body. When He was on the earth, He was shepherding. After His resurrection and ascension to the heavens, He is still shepherding.

When the Lord stayed with His disciples after His resurrection and before His ascension, in one of His appearings, He commissioned Peter to feed His lambs and shepherd His sheep in His absence, while He is in the heavens (John 21:15-17). Shepherding implies feeding, but it includes much more than feeding. To shepherd is to take all-inclusive tender care of the flock.

This is to incorporate the apostolic ministry with Christ's heavenly ministry to take care of God's flock, which is the church that issues in the Body of Christ. (*Crystallization-study of the Gospel of John,* pp. 130-131)

Today's Reading

Peter was self-confident in his natural strength and ability even to the point of thinking that he would follow the Lord both to prison and to death (Luke 22:33)....Peter was tested and he denied the Lord three times, even before a little maid (John 18:15-18, 25-27)....Peter was absolutely defeated and became a complete failure (Matt. 26:69-75). He did have a heart to love the Lord, but he was too confident in his own strength, his natural strength. His love for the Lord was precious, but his natural strength had to be denied and dealt with. The Lord allowed Peter to fail utterly in denying the Lord to His face three times, so that his natural strength and self-confidence could be dealt with.

Through his failure, Peter learned to serve the brothers by faith in the Lord and with humility (Luke 22:32; 1 Pet. 5:5-6). Peter was really broken and was turned from the natural ability to something in resurrection.

[We] all must learn this one lesson: to reject the natural strength and ability. Our natural strength and ability must be dealt with and put on the cross. Then [we] will be in resurrection and full of the divine element. Then whatever we do in the church service will be a ministry of the divine element to others. If our natural strength and ability are not dealt with, we will minister something natural to people by our church service. (*Basic Lessons on Service,* pp. 157-158)

In John 21:15 the Lord Jesus said to Simon Peter, "Simon, son of John, do you love Me more than these?" The Lord was here restoring Peter's love toward Him....[Then] the Lord Jesus charged him, saying, "Feed My lambs," "Shepherd My sheep," and "Feed My sheep." The first twenty chapters of the Gospel of John stress the matter of believing in the Son that we may have life (3:15). But in this chapter it is not a matter of believing but of loving. The fruit-bearing in chapter fifteen is the outflow of the riches of the inner life. Here the lamb-feeding is the nourishing with the riches of the inner life. In order to feed others we need to enjoy the riches of the Lord's divine life. This requires that we love Him. To believe in the Lord is to receive Him, and to love the Lord is to enjoy Him. The Lord came as life and as the life supply to us. We need to have faith in Him and love toward Him. According to the Gospel of John, these are the two requirements for participating in the Lord. (*Life-study of John,* pp. 585, 589)

Further Reading: Basic Lessons on Service, lsn. 20; *The Collected Works of Watchman Nee,* vol. 18, pp. 251-254; vol. 50, ch. 42; *Life-study of John,* msgs. 48-49

Enlightenment and inspiration: ______________

Morning Nourishment

John 15:5 I am the vine; you are the branches. He who abides in Me and I in him, he bears much fruit; for apart from Me you can do nothing.

When I first went to Taiwan, I thought nothing could be worked out there. At that time it was a desolate small island. One day the Lord told me to go along the railway from Taipei to visit the saints. After that visitation I was deeply impressed;...I picked up a burden and decided to begin the ministry there with a conference on August 1, 1949. About four or five hundred Christians from different denominations, who had escaped from mainland China to Taiwan, came on the first day of the conference. I said to them, "We are here to serve one kind of food—Christ. Please be clear about this. If you want anything else, you are wasting your time in coming here." Most of them did not come back. Only the real seekers came.

We took down their names and began to shepherd them. We distributed their names to different brothers and sisters to go and visit them. From the beginning of the work in Taiwan we practiced shepherding. When we had a big gospel meeting, we could get about five to six hundred names. Then we distributed all the names for the proper care. Most people want to have genuine, proper visitors. When we visit people, we should be genuine in our care for them. They will sense that we are not vain people. This shepherding way of preaching the gospel by visiting people warms them up. The church life in Taiwan began with about three or four hundred believers, but after four years we had forty thousand. Most of the people were not saved directly by my ministry; they were saved by the proper shepherding, the proper care. We all have to learn this. (*Crystallization-study of the Gospel of John,* pp. 134-135)

Today's Reading

Before I went to Taiwan in 1949, I was in Chefoo. I spoke each Lord's Day, and during the week I and an older brother went to visit the new ones. We were warmly welcomed by every family. They would gather their household together when we came. Within a short time, there was a real revival in Chefoo. The gospel was preached everywhere, not just by myself but by all the saints.

I also made the decision to set up a kitchen in the meeting hall, and I invited groups of twenty or thirty saints to eat together for fellowship. Within a little over half a year, I had invited all the members of the church. At that time there were at least five to six hundred saints in the church in Chefoo. This kind of shepherding stirred up the entire church. I hope the elders would use the hall as a dining room and invite the saints to come for fellowship. An elder should contact at least one person every day for the purpose of shepherding. We should also invite people to our homes for a meal, not inviting the familiar ones but the new ones. The revival in Chefoo occurred because of this kind of shepherding.

Shepherding works....The way that can save people effectively must be by small vital groups, and every one in this small vital group must be a shepherd. After a short time, the church will be revived. No other way is more prevailing than this shepherding way.

For the shepherding of the saints, there must be the healthy teaching in the vital groups. In 1 Timothy 3:2 Paul said that an elder should be apt to teach. Teaching here is similar to parents' teaching their children. An elder must be apt to render this kind of home teaching to the members of a local church. Then in 5:17 Paul said, "Let the elders who take the lead well be counted worthy of double honor, especially those who labor in word and teaching."

I hope that we would pray, "Lord, I want to be revived. From today I want to be a shepherd. I want to go to feed people, to shepherd people, and to flock people together."...We should learn to feed, to shepherd, and to flock together. All the churches have to learn how to flock together so that they can be blent together. In the atmosphere of flocking, people are subdued, convinced, nourished, and stirred up by the Lord. All the nearby churches should be flocked together for the saints to be shepherded and stirred up. (*Crystallization-study of the Gospel of John,* pp. 135-137)

Further Reading: Crystallization-study of the Gospel of John, ch. 13

Enlightenment and inspiration: ______________

Morning Nourishment

2 Cor. 3:6 Who has also made us sufficient as ministers of a new covenant, *ministers* not of the letter but of the Spirit; for the letter kills, but the Spirit gives life.

7:13 Because of this we have been comforted. And in addition to our comfort, we rejoiced more abundantly over the joy of Titus, because his spirit has been refreshed by all of you.

What we have in 2 Corinthians 7:2-16 is the intimate concern of the ministering life. Every believer who loves the Lord and who wants to come up to God's standard should become a minister of the new covenant. As long as we are believers in Christ, we should be…ministers of the new covenant, those who minister Christ as life so that the church may be built up as the Body of Christ. This ministry should be carried out not only by apostles and elders; it should be carried out by everyone in the church.

The goal of the Lord's recovery today is to recover this ministering of Christ by all the believers so that the church may be built up. This understanding is based on Paul's word in Ephesians 4, where he says that the apostles, prophets, evangelists, and shepherds and teachers perfect the saints unto the work of the ministry, unto the building up of the Body of Christ. For us all to be church builders, to minister Christ for the building up of the church, we need a ministering life.…We need to live a life of ministering Christ to others for the church. (*Life-study of 2 Corinthians,* pp. 379-380)

Today's Reading

The ministering life we see in 2 Corinthians is a fruitful life. We may be "spiritual," "holy," and "victorious" and yet not be fruitful. There are problems with that kind of spirituality, holiness, and victory. It is questionable whether those qualities are true and genuine.…According to the Bible, being spiritual is for the purpose of being fruitful. In the Gospel of John the Lord does not tell us to be spiritual, holy, and victorious. Rather, in John 15 He charges us to bear fruit, even to bear much fruit, abiding fruit. This is to live a ministering life.

It is possible to become knowledgeable in spiritual matters and powerful in preaching and yet still be unfruitful. In fact, instead of being fruitful and ministering life, such a person may cause others to suffer death.…Furthermore, in the shepherding of the saints, it is also possible that we may kill others. The reason for this killing, this fruitlessness, is the lack of intimate concern.

[Second Corinthians 7] reveals that we need an intimate concern. If we have ability to carry on a work but lack an intimate concern, our work will be fruitless. What is needed to establish a good family life and church life is intimate concern. How fruitful we are, how much fruit we bear, does not depend on what we are able to do. It depends on whether or not we have an intimate concern.

Brother Nee told us that in preaching the gospel we need to have a genuine concern for others. As long as we have the proper concern for people, we are well on our way to be qualified to be used of God for their salvation. A very good testimony of this is in the book *Seen and Heard.* In that book, the writer, James M'Kendrick, tells us of standing in front of a group of unbelievers and weeping, without saying a word. Nevertheless, a number were saved, for he had a deep concern. Eloquence, gift, and power can never touch people as deeply as your concern for them.

In 2 Corinthians 7 Paul was very emotional. In verse 13 he says that he "rejoiced more abundantly over the joy of Titus."… Paul was very human and emotional in his ministering of life… because his concern was so deep and intimate.…Do you know what a ministering life is? It is a life that warms up others. Learn to warm others. This is to have an intimate concern for them.

Many have read 2 Corinthians 7 without touching the matter of Paul's intimate concern. If we do not have this kind of concern for others, we shall not be fruitful. If I would minister life to the saints, I must have a genuine concern for them, a concern that is emotional, deep, and intimate. (*Life-study of 2 Corinthians,* pp. 380-384)

Further Reading: Life-study of 2 Corinthians, msg. 44

Enlightenment and inspiration: ______________

Morning Nourishment

1 Cor. 12:31 ...And moreover I show to you a most excellent way.

13:7 [Love] covers all things, believes all things, hopes all things, endures all things.

We all must learn to shepherd one another. This does not mean that since I am shepherding you, I do not need your shepherding. I need your shepherding. We all have defects and shortcomings. Everyone has defects. Therefore, we have to humble ourselves to meet God's grace. This strengthens our spirit to visit people and to take care of people regardless of whether they are good or bad. Regardless of what they are, we must go to visit them and keep visiting.... I am trying my best to help the church to build up the vital groups with such a shepherding spirit full of love and care for others.

We need to have this kind of love and go to tell all the dormant ones who think that the church condemns them that the church does not condemn anyone. Rather, the church wants to see all the dormant ones come back. If they all would come back, I would weep with tears of thanksgiving to the Lord. The Lord can testify for me that I do not condemn anyone. We have no qualification to condemn anyone. Without the Lord's mercy, we would be the same as the dormant ones. Therefore, we must love them...."Love covers all transgressions" (Prov. 10:12). (*A Word of Love to the Co-workers, Elders, Lovers, and Seekers of the Lord,* p. 32)

Today's Reading

The end of 1 Corinthians 12 reveals that love is the most excellent way (v. 31b). How can one be an elder...[or] a co-worker? Love is the most excellent way. How do we shepherd people? Love is the most excellent way. Love is the most excellent way for us to prophesy and to teach others. Love is the most excellent way for us to be anything or do anything.

Love prevails. We should love everybody, even our enemies. If the co-workers and elders do not love the bad ones, eventually they will have nothing to do. We must be perfect as our Father is perfect (Matt. 5:48) by loving the evil ones and the good ones without any discrimination. We must be perfect as our Father because we are His sons, His species. This is most crucial. How can we be a co-worker and an elder? It is by love in every way. We must love any kind of person. The Lord Jesus said that He came to be a Physician, not for the healthy ones, but for the sick ones. The Lord said, "Those who are strong have no need of a physician, but those who are ill" (Matt. 9:12).

The church is not a police station to arrest people or a law court to judge people, but a home to raise up the believers. Parents know that the worse their children are, the more they need their raising up. If our children were angels, they would not need our parenting to raise them up. The church is a loving home to raise up the children. The church is also a hospital to heal and to recover the sick ones. Finally, the church is a school to teach and edify the unlearned ones who do not have much understanding. Because the church is a home, a hospital, and a school, the co-workers and elders should be one with the Lord to raise up, to heal, to cover, and to teach others in love.

Some of the churches, however, are police stations to arrest the sinful ones and law courts to judge them. Paul's attitude was different. He said, "Who is weak, and I am not weak?" (2 Cor. 11:29a). When the scribes and Pharisees brought an adulterous woman to the Lord, He said to them, "He who is without sin among you, let him be the first to throw a stone at her" (John 8:7). After all of them left, the Lord asked the sinful woman, "Woman, where are they? Has no one condemned you?" She said, "No one, Lord." Then Jesus said, "Neither do I condemn you" (vv. 10-11). Who is without sin? Who is perfect? Paul said, "To the weak I became weak that I might gain the weak" (1 Cor. 9:22). This is love. We should not consider that others are weak but we are not. This is not love. Love covers and builds up, so love is the most excellent way for us to be anything and to do anything for the building up of the Body of Christ. (*The Vital Groups,* pp. 74-75)

Further Reading: The Vital Groups, ch. 8; *A Word of Love to the Co-workers, Elders, Lovers, and Seekers of the Lord,* ch. 2

Enlightenment and inspiration: ______________

____

____

____

Hymns, #922

1 To the lost world minister Christ,
Not just by word, but by life,
Imparting Christ by living deeds
To the poor souls living in strife.

To the lost world minister Christ,
By daily walk making Him known;
Imparting Christ by whom you live,
Share with all men what you own.

2 To the lost world minister Christ,
The precious One you possess,
Imparting Christ to those you love
As all their gain and success.

3 To the lost world minister Christ,
The very Christ you enjoy,
Imparting Christ to all your friends
As all their boast and their joy.

4 To the lost world minister Christ,
Who is your life and your all,
Imparting Christ to all you meet,
All fallen ones, great or small.

Composition for prophecy with main point and sub-points:

Shepherding the Flock of God (1)
The Pattern of the Apostle Paul in Shepherding

Scripture Reading: Acts 20:17-36; Phil. 3:17; 1 Thes. 1:5; 2 Thes. 3:9; 1 Tim. 1:16

Day 1

I. In the church the most important thing is the person (2 Tim. 2:20-22):

A. The importance of the person far exceeds that of the work; what we are is more important than what we do.

B. We cannot serve God beyond what we are as a person.

C. The kind of person we are determines the kind of fruit we produce (Matt. 7:17-18).

D. If our person is wrong, we may build up something by what we do but tear down more by what we are.

E. If a person's heart is right, the person is right (5:8; 2 Cor. 6:11; 7:3):

1. God pays much attention to man's heart (Isa. 29:13).

2. Whether or not we can become a blessing to others depends on our heart:

a. If we are a proper person, wherever we go, we will become a blessing there.

b. If a person's heart is not right, even if he were to accomplish monumental works, others will still not receive the blessing.

3. The heart only deals with the question of being for God or not for God:

a. The heart must be set on God instead of on the works (Matt. 5:8).

b. Many things in the church life can turn our heart away from the Lord.

F. In serving the Lord, we have to pay attention to the person and not merely to doing the right things.

Day 2

II. The best way to shepherd others, to cherish and nourish them, is to give them a proper

pattern (Acts 20:28; 1 Thes. 2:1-12; 2 Cor. 1:12—2:14; 11:28-29; 1 Cor. 9:22):

A. Many Christians today have no sense of direction, because they do not have a proper pattern (Matt. 9:36; 15:14).

B. The proper way to take care of the new believers and the young ones is to show them a pattern; by showing them a pattern, we water them, nourish them, and cherish them (Phil. 3:17; 2 Thes. 3:9; 1 Tim. 1:16; 4:12; Titus 2:7; 1 Pet. 5:3).

C. Paul fed his spiritual children with his living of Christ; this is why he emphasized his manner of life when he was with them (1 Thes. 1:5; 2:1-12).

Day 3 **III. To the elders of the church in Ephesus, Paul was a pattern; thus, he could remind the elders of how he was with them all the time (Acts 20:18, 35):**

A. The shepherding of God's flock was on Paul's heart (v. 28):

1. Paul did not consider that he was doing a great work; rather, he considered what he did as shepherding the flock of God.
2. We need to be revolutionized in our logic and consideration and not think that we are going to do a great work for Christ, like certain spiritual giants who actually did not accomplish much for God's interest but instead made a name for themselves, with little result for the building up of the Body of Christ.

B. Paul was a pattern to the believers of living and ministering Christ as the Spirit in his spirit for the building up of the Body of Christ (1 Tim. 1:16; 4:12; Rom. 8:16):

1. Paul lived by the Spirit, walked by the Spirit, sowed unto the Spirit, and ministered the Spirit as a spiritual man who lived and served in his spirit (Gal. 5:16, 25; 6:8; 2 Cor. 3:6; 1 Cor. 2:15; 2 Cor. 2:13; Rom. 1:9; 8:16).

2. Paul lived and did everything in the Body, through the Body, and for the Body (12:4-5; 1 Cor. 12:12-27; Eph. 4:1-6, 15-16; Col. 2:19).

Day 4 & Day 5

C. Paul served the Lord as a slave; he regarded himself as a slave of Christ Jesus (Acts 20:19; Rom. 1:1):

1. Paul's use of the term *a slave of Christ Jesus* indicates that he was not a self-appointed apostle or one hired by the Lord.
2. Paul was one purchased to serve God and minister to His people, not in the natural life but in the regenerated life (Exo. 21:6; Matt. 20:26; 25:14).

D. Paul was a person in spirit; as such a person, he had an open spirit, a frank spirit, a pure spirit, a bold spirit, a humble spirit, a loving spirit, a tender spirit, a spirit that was not self-seeking, and a coordinating spirit (Acts 20:22).

E. Paul lived and moved in and with the Divine Trinity, and he ministered the processed Triune God as grace (vv. 21-24, 28, 32, 35).

F. Paul declared "all the counsel of God," not withholding anything that was profitable (vv. 20, 26-27).

G. Paul testified repentance unto God and faith in the Lord Jesus Christ (v. 21).

H. Paul testified of the gospel of the grace of God and proclaimed the kingdom (vv. 24-25).

I. Paul did not consider his soul-life precious to himself but was burdened to finish the course and the ministry he had received (v. 24).

Day 6

J. Paul did not covet but worked with his own hands in order to meet his needs and to give to others, supporting the weak (vv. 33-35):

1. In order to be a proper pattern, we need to be pure in our motives, especially concerning money.
2. If we are not pure concerning money, if we are not sincere, honest, and faithful

regarding it, we may be among those who adulterate the word of God and peddle it (2 Cor. 2:17).

3. An impure motive may cause us to use flattery or to have a pretext for covetousness (1 Thes. 2:5).

K. Paul taught the believers publicly and from house to house, admonishing each one with tears (Acts 20:19-20, 31).

L. Paul committed the saints to God and to the word of His grace, which is able to build them up and to give them the inheritance among all those who have been sanctified (v. 32).

M. We need to contact people, sinners and believers, and take care of their needs as the apostle Paul did (2 Cor. 1:12—2:14; 11:28-29; 1 Cor. 9:22).

Morning Nourishment

Matt. 7:18 **A good tree cannot produce bad fruit, neither can a corrupt tree produce good fruit.**

2 Tim. 2:20-21 **But in a great house there are not only gold and silver vessels but also wooden and earthen; and some are unto honor, and some unto dishonor. If therefore anyone cleanses himself from these, he will be a vessel unto honor, sanctified, useful to the master, prepared unto every good work.**

We all know that to do anything, first there is the need of a person to do it. Next comes the method. The Chinese say that the kind of thing accomplished depends on the kind of person carrying it out. The method may be the same. But for you to do it, it will succeed. For me to do it, it may fail. For you, there may be a good result. For me, the result may not be very good. Hence, the problem is not the method but the person. Concerning the administration of the church by the elders, our emphasis is also not the method of administration. Rather it is the administrator that is important. It does not mean that with the right method the church will be managed well. Only when the person is right will the church be managed well. Hence, the foremost question is the person; the methods are secondary. Without the administrating person, the method amounts to zero. Only when there is the administrating person, plus the methods, will the result be beneficial. The person is the basis.

This shows us that whoever tries to consider the management of the church from the standpoint of methods is wrong. The matter must begin from the person of the elders. It is useless to change the method; the only way is to change the person. (*The Elders' Management of the Church,* pp. 25-26)

Today's Reading

I would seriously warn the brothers that to manage affairs in the church, it is dangerous to use any method when the person is not right. What are methods? To put it in terms that are not so nice, methods are crafts. To be crafty is to be political. To administrate a church, you cannot be political. The work of all those who manage the church in a political way will result in vanity. The worldly politicians can play politics, but the elders in the church cannot play politics. The church is not a society; the church is a family. In a family, the head of the household cannot be crafty or play politics. The head of the household manages the family by his person. It is the person that manages the family, not a method that does it. In the same way, the church is the house of God. There is no need for a good method of administration; rather, there is the need of a good person for administration.

If we do not have the proper person, or if the person is not the right person, we cannot expect things to be done well. ...We have to see that the administration in the church depends firstly on the person. We are not saying that methods are not important, but methods depend upon the person. If the person is off, methods are of no use, no matter how good they may be. The person must be right before the methods will work.

In addition to the problem of the person, there is also the problem of the heart, which also needs much dealing. Whereas in the world it is possible to consider only the person, in the church there must be a certain standard with regard to the heart as well. The reason for this is that in the church everything is transparent and in the light. There cannot be any inconsistency between the outward condition and the inward condition. Strictly speaking, even in the world, for a person to be right, he must have a very proper heart. This shows the absolute relatedness between the heart and the person. (*The Elders' Management of the Church*, pp. 26-27, 37)

Further Reading: The Elders' Management of the Church, ch. 2; *Watchman Nee—A Seer of the Divine Revelation in the Present Age,* ch. 11; *The Collected Works of Watchman Nee,* vol. 57, ch. 10

Enlightenment and inspiration: ______________

Morning Nourishment

Phil. 3:17 **Be imitators together of me, brothers, and observe those who thus walk even as you have us as a pattern.**

1 Tim. 1:16 **...That in me, the foremost, Jesus Christ might display all His long-suffering for a pattern to those who are to believe on Him unto eternal life.**

4:12 **Let no one despise your youth, but be a pattern to the believers in word, in conduct, in love, in faith, in purity.**

1 Pet. 5:3 **Nor as lording it over your allotments but by becoming patterns of the flock.**

[In 1 Thessalonians 2 Paul] gives a strong testimony of his living among the Thessalonians. He reminds them of the apostles coming and of their manner of life among them.... [Paul] emphasized [this] because he was presenting a pattern of a proper living to the young saints. I hope that all the elders and leading ones will see from Paul's example that we must be a pattern to the saints. In every local church there must be some patterns, some models, for others to follow.

In 1:6 Paul says to the Thessalonians, "And you became imitators of us and of the Lord." Imitating is related to growing. In fact, in many ways to imitate is to grow. In a family children imitate their parents and older brothers and sisters. The little ones do not invent anything; instead, they imitate others....A child learns the language spoken by his parents...with the same accent...by imitation....In a family to imitate actually means to grow. The children imitate their parents in many things—in gestures, in speech, and even in character. Parents are patterns, models, for their children. Whatever the parents are, the children will be also. (*Life-study of 1 Thessalonians,* pp. 109-110)

Today's Reading

To give the new believers and young ones a lot of teaching is not the proper way to take care of them. The proper way to foster them is to show them a pattern. By showing them a pattern you water them, supply them, nourish them, and cherish them. This is fostering. If you find that your experience is somewhat lacking, point the new believers to different people in the Bible....We can present the lives of Bible characters in such a way as to foster the growth of the young ones.

If we give too much teaching to new ones and young ones, we shall damage them. Every mother knows that one of the most important matters in the raising of children is proper feeding. Caring for children is ninety percent a matter of feeding and ten percent a matter of teaching. This also should be our practice in caring for new believers in the church. We must learn to have ninety percent feeding and ten percent teaching. Feeding involves the presenting of patterns either from the Bible or from church history. By reading the biographies of saints throughout the ages, we nourish ourselves and experience a kind of fostering. The point here is that the best way to feed others and foster them is to give them a proper pattern. If there is no pattern, there can be no fostering. Only by having a pattern can we feed others.

In the book of 1 Thessalonians Paul was not preaching himself. Rather, he was feeding his spiritual children with his own living of Christ. This means that Paul's way of living was used to feed his spiritual children. This was the reason he emphasized his coming to the Thessalonians, his preaching, his way of handling the word of God, and his manner of living.

Today...many Christians have no sense of direction. The reason for this lack of direction is that they do not have a proper pattern. We need to be a pattern to others and foster them, cherishing them as mothers and exhorting them as fathers to walk worthily of God....To walk worthily of God is actually to live God. Only a life that lives God is worthy of God. When we live God, we walk worthily of Him. Such a walk will lead us into the kingdom and usher us into the glory of God. This is the goal of God's calling. God has called us to enter His kingdom and glory. (*Life-study of 1 Thessalonians,* pp. 110, 105)

Further Reading: Life-study of 1 Thessalonians, msg. 13; *Life-study of 1 Timothy,* pp. 13-16; *Life-study of Philippians,* msg. 43

Enlightenment and inspiration: ______________

Morning Nourishment

Acts 20:18 ...You yourselves know, from the first day that I set foot in Asia, how I was with you all the time.

28 Take heed to yourselves and to all the flock, among whom the Holy Spirit has placed you as overseers to shepherd the church of God, which He obtained through His own blood.

35 In all things I have shown you by example that toiling in this way we ought to support the weak and to remember the words of the Lord Jesus, that He Himself said, It is more blessed to give than to receive.

Without shepherding, there is no way for us to minister life to others....We need to contact and take care of others, sinners and believers, as the apostle Paul...did in contacting people and taking care of people's need (2 Cor. 1:23—2:14). In 2 Corinthians 11:28-29 Paul said, "Apart from the things,...there is this: the crowd of cares pressing upon me daily, the anxious concern for all the churches. Who is weak, and I am not weak? Who is stumbled, and I myself do not burn?" This unveils the care of a proper shepherd.

Acts 20 says that while Paul was on his way to Jerusalem, he sent word to Ephesus and called for the elders of the church. He told them that they should shepherd God's flock, which God purchased with His own blood (v. 28). The shepherding of God's flock was on Paul's heart. Many think that Paul was a great apostle doing a great work as a great career. But Paul considered what he did as shepherding the flock of God. We have to be revolutionized in our logic and consideration. We should not think that we are going to do a great work for Christ like certain spiritual giants. These so-called giants actually did not accomplish much for God's interest. Instead, they only made a name for themselves with little result for the building up of the Body of Christ. (*The Vital Groups*, pp. 61-62)

Today's Reading

Paul is a real pattern to all of the elders....Although he himself had never been an elder, yet he set up a model, a pattern, an example for the elders whom he had trained. So, whatever he spoke about himself, his expectation was that all the elders would follow his steps and imitate what he had been doing....[Paul] was serving the Lord as a slave. The elders all have to serve the Lord as a slave. They are not put into a position of dignity or rank. In the church there is no rank and no position. There is only humility and slavery.

Among us in the past our concept was that the elders only manage the church affairs, make decisions, and give announcements. But we have to realize that to manage the business affairs of the church is secondary....The main responsibility of the elders is firstly to shepherd [1 Pet. 5:2]....As we have indicated, shepherding requires teaching, so the elders should also teach (1 Tim. 3:2; 5:17). For the elders to teach others, they first of all must be taught. They must learn first.

Just to visit the homes of the saints and tell them to trust in the Lord and believe in Him is not adequate. The elders must read to them some profitable verses, give them some definitions, and teach them with the holy Word. Then they will be edified, established, strengthened, and built up.

To shepherd is not just to give a message. This is neither adequate nor primary. The primary responsibility is to go to the saints and shepherd them in their homes. So Paul set up a pattern for the elders by teaching the saints publicly and from house to house....If there is a house, the elders should go. If there are ten houses, they should go to each one to visit each of the saints....Close to fifty years ago, I spent much time visiting people for the gospel to get them saved and going to the saints' homes. By visiting a home the real situation of that person's environment could be seen. Then the elders could render them the proper shepherding....We should save...[our] time to shepherd the saints. If we go to the homes of the saints to shepherd them, there will be a record of this in the heavens. (*Talks concerning the Church Services, Part One,* pp. 15-18)

Further Reading: The Vital Groups, msgs. 6-7

Enlightenment and inspiration: ______________

Morning Nourishment

Acts 20:19-20 Serving the Lord as a slave with all humility and tears and trials which came upon me by the plots of the Jews; how I did not withhold any of those things that are profitable by not declaring *them* to you and by *not* teaching you publicly and from house to house.

27 For I did not shrink from declaring to you all the counsel of God.

Elders should serve the Lord not just as servants, but slaves, losing their right and all kinds of liberty. Actually, to be put into the eldership is to be brought into slavery. We all are slaves to serve the Lord. To serve the Lord here is not to serve the Lord directly, but indirectly by serving His people. The elders must pick up the burden of a slave to serve the big family of their Master. We must behave, do things, and even have our being as slaves with all humility.

We have no right to be proud of anything. Everything that is glorious should go to our Master. He is the only One who is qualified to be proud of anything. We are destined to be humble. To be humble is not an easy thing; to be proud is easy. To be humble and even to be humbled is not a happy thing, but a thing of tears.

For the elders never to drop tears for the saints under their care might not be so good. Tears should go along with our humility. We should be humbled by the situation and ready to accept the trials from others. (*Talks concerning the Church Services, Part One,* p. 16)

Today's Reading

Paul was serving the Lord as a slave with all humility and tears because at his time there were others competing with him. They even plotted to undermine his work, his ministry, and himself. So, trials followed.

The elders should not anticipate much comfort but be prepared to face sufferings and trials. On the one hand, we all must pick up the burden of the eldership. Yet, on the other hand, we must be ready to face any kind of trials that come upon us from others. At Paul's time the trials came from the Jews who were not atheists, but those who worshipped God, and, in their view, served God.

[Then in Acts 20:20 we see that] Paul did not shrink from his duty. He did not withdraw from declaring to the saints anything that was profitable to them....Paul did a faithful job to declare every bit of God's interests that He had toward His people. Paul did not withdraw from his responsibility. Rather, he taught the believers publicly in the meetings and privately from house to house.

From now on the elders should do more home visitation. By visiting the homes of the saints, the elders can teach and shepherd the saints. Teaching in this verse really means shepherding. In the New Testament, teaching goes along with the matter of shepherding. Shepherding needs the proper teaching.

In Acts 20:27 Paul continues to say, "For I did not shrink from declaring to you all the counsel of God." Not only did Paul teach them, care for their interests, and care for the things that were profitable to them, but he declared also God's counsel, God's plan, and God's economy. No doubt, Paul taught the Ephesians a great deal concerning God's New Testament economy.

Similarly all the elders must learn what God's New Testament economy is and point this out to the saints. By knowing God's eternal economy, most of the saints would then be solidly grounded and deeply rooted....What is needed among us is the proper biblical, divine revelation concerning God's eternal economy.

The elders must learn all the things of God's economy and dive into them. By so doing they will pick up a real burden. They will be able to comfort the disappointed saints by telling them God's economy. To hear God's economy and receive such a high calling will become a strong comfort and encouragement to the disappointed ones. The problems that we are facing today in the recovery are mainly due to the lack of a deep understanding and realization of God's eternal economy. (*Talks concerning the Church Services, Part One*, pp. 16-19)

Further Reading: Talks concerning the Church Services, Part One, chs. 2-3; *Life-study of Acts,* msg. 53

Enlightenment and inspiration: ______________________

____

____

____

Morning Nourishment

Acts 20:22 And now, behold, I am going bound in the spirit to Jerusalem, not knowing what will meet me there.

2 Cor. 12:18-19 I entreated Titus and sent with *him* the brother. Titus did not take advantage of you, did he? Did we not walk in the same spirit? In the same steps? All this time you have been thinking that we are defending ourselves to you. Before God in Christ we speak; but all things, beloved, *are* for your building up.

This man Paul has an open spirit. It is not easy to have an open spirit. On the contrary, it is easy for us to close our spirit, to shut our spirit up. It could be that most of the time we are closed in our spirit. The more we are fallen, the more we are closed in our spirit; the more we are delivered, the more we are saved, the more we are open in the spirit. For the church life we need an open spirit.

You may open your mind, open your emotion, and even open your entire heart, yet you would still not open your spirit to others. When you open your spirit, you are fully, thoroughly open to others. (*An Autobiography of a Person in the Spirit,* p. 74)

Today's Reading

In the church life we should not lose our temper, but we have to be frank with one another. We should not be political in the church life, but should always say something to a brother's face. We should not be backbiters (Rom. 1:30; Gal. 5:15). The apostle Paul was a frank person with a frank spirit, and we need to be the same.

The apostle Paul was also one who had a pure spirit. If you never say anything, it is easy for others to think that you are pure. But once you begin to speak, either your purity or lack of purity becomes manifested. In 2 Corinthians the apostle Paul opened himself up and spoke many things, yet we are impressed with how pure his spirit is.…We have to be frank, but if we are going to be frank we have to be pure. A frank spirit has to be matched with a pure spirit. If you are not pure, your frankness will damage me.

Paul spoke bold words, but his words were full of a loving spirit. Paul's spirit was a loving spirit, a spirit always stretching out to love others, to take care of others. I do not mean that we need a love which has its source in our emotions, but we need a loving spirit, a spirit within us that always loves others.

Another characteristic of Paul's spirit is that his spirit was tender. You can speak boldly in words, yet still with a tender spirit. We need to be dealt with by the working of the cross so that we can be a person with a tender spirit like the apostle Paul.

Paul's spirit was not self-seeking. Second Corinthians shows us that he had a spirit that never sought anything for himself. He had a spirit fully, wholly, and thoroughly delivered out of the self. Whatever his spirit sought was for the good of the church and for the interest of Christ. Such a spirit is greatly needed in today's church life.

The final characteristic of Paul's spirit is that his spirit was always coordinating with others. Our spirit might be tender, pure, and loving, yet not so cooperating or coordinating with other saints. The verses in the Scripture reading show us that Paul's spirit was always coordinating with his co-workers, coordinating with the local churches, and even coordinating with those believers who did not treat him so well. He was coordinating all the time, trying to be one with the saints, one with the local churches, and one with the co-workers. He was so coordinating in the spirit.

These are the real characteristics of a person's spirit who lives in the Holy of Holies. We need such a spirit for the building up of the Lord's Body. Without such a balanced, adjusted spirit, the church life could never be realized by you regardless of how many doctrines and how much knowledge you possess. For us to realize the church life, we need such a balanced and adjusted spirit. May we all look to the Lord that we may have such a spirit. (*An Autobiography of a Person in the Spirit,* pp. 75-79)

Further Reading: An Autobiography of a Person in the Spirit, ch. 9; *To Serve in the Human Spirit,* ch. 4

Enlightenment and inspiration: ______________

____

____

____

Morning Nourishment

Acts 20:31-34 **Therefore watch, remembering that for three years, night and day, I did not cease admonishing each one with tears. And now I commit you to God and to the word of His grace, which is able to build *you* up and to give *you* the inheritance among all those who have been sanctified. I have coveted no one's silver or gold or clothing. You yourselves know that these hands have ministered to my needs and to those who are with me.**

[In Acts 20:31 and 32] Paul commits the believers to God and to the word of His grace. Grace is the Triune God received and enjoyed by the believers. I believe that during the three years Paul was in Ephesus, he daily spoke the word of God's grace to the saints. (*Life-study of Acts,* p. 477)

Today's Reading

We can testify that, by the Lord's mercy, the word of God's grace can be found in the Life-study messages....I would encourage the young people to take the time over the next several years to become constituted of all the Life-study messages. If the young people are saturated with these messages in the coming years, saturated with the word concerning God's New Testament economy, many will be useful in serving the Lord full time. They will be able to go to other cities and countries and convey to others God's New Testament economy.

Even those who are much older still have the time to be constituted of these messages and then have years to serve the Lord by carrying out God's New Testament economy throughout the earth.

In Acts 20:32 we see the function of the word of God's grace. First, this word is able to build up the saints. To build up the saints requires the growth in the divine life, and the growth in the divine life needs the nourishment of the divine element and the edification and equipment with the divine knowledge. All these can be afforded only by the word of God's abundant grace, which is the Triune God Himself who went through all the processes of incarnation, human living, crucifixion, resurrection, and ascension and who has been given to the saints for their enjoyment.

Second, the word of God's grace functions to give us "the inheritance among all those who have been sanctified." The divine inheritance is the Triune God Himself with all that He has, all He has done, and all He will do for His redeemed people. This Triune God is embodied in the all-inclusive Christ (Col. 2:9), who is the portion allotted to the saints as their inheritance (Col. 1:12). The Holy Spirit, who has been given to the saints, is the foretaste, the pledge, and the guarantee of this divine inheritance (Rom. 8:23; Eph. 1:14), which we are sharing and enjoying today in God's New Testament jubilee as the foretaste and will share and enjoy in full in the coming age and for eternity (1 Pet. 1:4).

On the day we were regenerated, we were given the right to share an inheritance. This inheritance includes all the blessings related to eternal life. Daily we need to take possession of this inheritance and enjoy it. This inheritance is legal, proper, and legitimate, for Christ died to purchase it for us, paying the price of His precious blood. Daily we may participate in and enjoy the inheritance that is ours today and for eternity.

To participate in God's inheritance requires us to be sanctified, and to be sanctified requires the word of God's grace.

Paul worked with his hands at making tents (Acts 18:3) in order to support both himself and those who were with him [20:33-34]. He worked in order to help his young co-workers. This indicates that Paul's way was not that of today's clergy who make a profession out of preaching.

Like Paul, we all should bear the New Testament economy wherever we may be. If the situation allows, we may spend our full time in the work of the ministry. Otherwise, we should do something to support ourselves and also to help others. (*Life-study of Acts,* pp. 477-479)

Further Reading: Life-study of Acts, msg. 55; *Further Light concerning the Building Up of the Body of Christ,* ch. 2

Enlightenment and inspiration: ______________

Hymns, #1245

1 When the brothers are in order,
And you sense Christ is their life,
Follow them and watch for Jesus,
Ending thus your thought and strife.

Follow brothers, follow sisters,
When you sense Christ is their life,
Follow brothers, follow sisters,
Help prepare the Bride for Christ.

2 When you follow, as you follow,
Take the blood, and call His name;
Much assurance He will give you,
And the enemy you'll shame.

3 When they speak, as they are speaking,
Open wide your heart to them,
Thus the Word of God receiving,
Word of God, and not of men.

4 Now the Word of God is running,
Running fast, and running free.
This is how the Lord is moving,
In His own recovery.

5 O be glad, rejoice, dear brothers,
For the coming wedding day.
Then the Bride will be made ready—
Those who followed all the way.

Composition for prophecy with main point and sub-points:

Shepherding the Flock of God (2)
The Charge of the Apostle Paul concerning Shepherding

Scripture Reading: Acts 20:28-31

Day 1

I. "From Miletus he [Paul] sent word to Ephesus and called for the elders of the church" (Acts 20:17):

A. The term *elders* indicates something organic, something of life; an elder is a person who is mature in life.

B. The function of the elders must be something of the Spirit organically (1 Cor. 12:4-7, 28; Rom. 12:8):

1. If the elders take the lead in an organizational way, this indicates that the church has degraded.
2. If the elders live in the spirit by life to nourish, cherish, and shepherd the church, they are not organizational but organic.

Day 2

II. "Take heed to yourselves and to all the flock, among whom the Holy Spirit has placed you as overseers to shepherd the church of God, which He obtained through His own blood" (Acts 20:28):

A. Paul charged the elders to watch and take heed to themselves and to all the flock (vv. 31, 28):

1. The elders need to pay close attention to themselves and to their teaching, holding to the faithful word, which is according to the apostles' teaching, that they may be able to stop troublesome talkers, calm a tumultuous situation, and fulfill their duty in teaching (1 Tim. 4:16; 3:2; 5:17; Titus 1:9-14).
2. "There shall be one flock, one Shepherd" (John 10:16):

a. The one flock signifies the one church, the one Body of Christ, brought forth by the Lord's eternal, divine life, which He imparted into His members through His death (vv. 10-18; Eph. 2:14-16; 3:6).

b. The Lord's sheep have received the divine life, and by the divine life the sheep live together as one flock.

c. The one flock is not an organization—it is a flocking together in life to be the organic Body of Christ.

d. This one flock is the one universal church, the Body of Christ; it no longer belongs to the Jewish fold or the Gentile world but stands by itself as the church of God set apart from the Jews and the Gentiles (1 Cor. 10:32).

e. The local churches are the flock of God, His possession, allotted to the elders for their care (1 Pet. 5:2-3).

Day 3

B. Paul told the elders that it was the Holy Spirit who had placed them among the flock as overseers (Acts 20:28):

1. The apostles appointed the elders in every church (14:23), but in 20:28 Paul says that the Holy Spirit had placed the elders as overseers to shepherd the church; this indicates that the Holy Spirit was one with the apostles in their appointing of the elders and that the apostles did it according to the leading of the Holy Spirit.

2. From Paul's word we see that the existence of the churches is altogether due to the Holy Spirit, not due to the apostles; because the Holy Spirit establishes the elders, it is the Holy Spirit who establishes the churches.

C. Paul charged the elders to shepherd the church of God (v. 28):

1. Although a local church needs administration and management in its business

affairs, the main responsibility of the elders is to shepherd (1 Pet. 5:2):

a. The local church is like a flock, and the elders are the shepherds to shepherd this flock, taking care of the situation of the flock and meeting the needs.

b. The responsibility of the elders as overseers is not to rule over others but to shepherd them, to take all-inclusive tender care of the flock.

Day 4

2. The elders should shepherd the church and take care of the church according to the apostles' teaching (Acts 2:42; Titus 1:9):

a. The elders should never separate themselves from the apostles' teaching.

b. The elders take the lead to put the apostles' teaching into practice.

3. Shepherding requires teaching, so the elders should teach; for the elders to teach others, they must learn first.

Day 5

D. Paul reminded the elders that the church was precious to God, for He had obtained it through His own blood (Acts 20:28):

1. Paul's word here indicates the precious love of God for the church and the preciousness, the exceeding worth, of the church in the eyes of God.

2. Paul expected that the elders as overseers would treasure the church, as God does.

3. As those appointed by God to care for the flock of God, the elders need to love the church.

4. In taking care of a church, we should never take the way of legality but the way of love, the only way which builds up the church (1 Cor. 12:31b—13:13; 8:1).

Day 6

III. "I know that after my departure fierce wolves will come in among you, not sparing the flock. And from among you yourselves

men will rise up, speaking perverted things to draw away the disciples after them" (Acts 20:29-30):

A. To spare the flock is to love the flock with tender care by cherishing and nourishing; the wolves, who are hunting for prey, do not care for the flock in this way but sacrifice the church for their own interests and satisfaction.

B. The perverted ones among the believers in the church are always used by the devil, who hates the church, to draw the sheep away after them to form another flock.

Morning Nourishment

Acts 20:17 And from Miletus he sent *word* to Ephesus and called for the elders of the church.

1 Cor. 12:28 And God has placed some in the church: first apostles, second prophets, third teachers; then works of power, then gifts of healing, helps, administrations, *various* kinds of tongues.

4 But there are distinctions of gifts, but the same Spirit.

In Peter's first Epistle, he spoke to his fellow elders. Peter was an elder in Jerusalem. He charged the elders to shepherd the flock of God (1 Pet. 5:1-2). The word *shepherd* nearly equals the two words *nourish* and *cherish.* A good shepherd always loves the flock, and the flock eventually loves this shepherd. They know each other intimately. To shepherd is not to control. In John 21 the Lord asked Peter, "Do you love Me?" Then He indicated that if Peter loved Him, he would feed His sheep and shepherd His sheep (vv. 15-17). The Lord Jesus spoke this to show how we should take care of the church. We should be those who are one with Him to feed, shepherd, nourish, and cherish the church. This is the organic way to care for the church. (*Elders' Training, Book 9: The Eldership and the God-ordained Way (1),* p. 75)

Today's Reading

The leading ones' care for the church is not an organizational matter. The church is not an organization. The church is God's family, God's household (Eph. 2:19; Gal. 6:10). All the elders should be the teaching fathers and the nourishing mothers (1 Thes. 2:7, 11). This is the way to take care of the church. It is altogether an organic matter, not organizational. The term *elder* also indicates something organic, something of life. An elder is a person who is mature in life.

To see more concerning the organic service in the Body of Christ, let us read 1 Corinthians 12:28 [above]... *Administrations* refers to the eldership in the church. *Helps* refers to the services of the deacons and deaconesses (1 Tim. 3:8-13). Administrations and helps are listed with apostles, with prophets, with teachers, and with works of power, healing, and tongues. This proves that both the helps by the deacons and the administration by the elders are not organizational. They are from the Spirit.

According to our natural thought, the government of the church has nothing to do with the distribution of gifts by the Spirit. But 1 Corinthians 12 tells us clearly that even the service of the deacons as helps and the function of the elders as administrations are distributions of gifts by the Spirit. This has to be something of the Spirit organically, not something of organization....The administration by the elders...is a gift from the Spirit. Since this is the case, it has to be organic.

The spiritual gifts are of two categories—the miraculous gifts and the gifts of life given according to grace. Romans 12:6 speaks of the gifts of life given according to grace. These gifts are the issue of the development of our spiritual function in the spiritual life. In 1 Corinthians 12:28 Paul puts the gifts of life and the miraculous gifts together. Helps and administrations are gifts of life. Since they are gifts, they are something of the Spirit, and they are organic.

In Romans 12:8 Paul refers to taking the lead as a gift according to grace. This refers to the elders in the church. To lead in the church is to administrate. We may consider that the administration of the church...is altogether a positional, organizational matter. But Romans 12 tells us that to lead, to administrate, to function as an elder in the church, is one of the gifts given according to grace. This indicates that the leading of the elders is organic. It is by life and not organizational. These three words—*eldership, administration,* and *lead*—are misunderstood by Christians as something organizational. After much study of the Word, we can see that they are not organizational. They are organic. (*Elders' Training, Book 9: The Eldership and the God-ordained Way (1),* pp. 75-77)

Further Reading: Elders' Training, Book 9: The Eldership and the God-ordained Way (1), chs. 4, 6

Enlightenment and inspiration: ______________

Morning Nourishment

1 Tim. 3:2 The overseer then must be without reproach, the husband of one wife, temperate, of a sober mind, orderly, hospitable, apt to teach.

4:6 If you lay these things before the brothers, you will be a good minister of Christ Jesus, being nourished with the words of the faith and of the good teaching which you have closely followed.

16 Take heed to yourself and to your teaching; continue in these things; for in doing this you will save both yourself and those who hear you.

In 1 Timothy 3:2 Paul says that an elder should be apt to teach. To teach here is similar to parents teaching their children. An elder must be apt to render this kind of home teaching to the members of the local church.

If a parent has not received a proper education, it will be difficult for him to teach his children. Likewise, if the elders would be apt to teach, they need to be knowledgeable....If a brother is not knowledgeable concerning the truth, he is disqualified from the eldership. An elder should be able to teach the saints like a parent helps a child with his homework. However, this does not mean that every elder should be a teacher. It is not necessary for parents to be teachers in order to help their children with homework. Similarly, not all elders are teachers, but they all should be apt to teach. (*Life-study of 1 Timothy,* pp. 45-46)

Today's Reading

If you have a heart to care for others in the Lord's recovery, you should not give them mere teaching. Whenever you fellowship with others concerning Christ, you may give them some knowledge. But while you are teaching them, you need to exercise your spirit to minister spiritual food that they may be nourished. If you do this, you will be a good minister of Christ.

With Paul and Timothy we see an excellent pattern....Paul told Timothy to lay "these things before the brothers" [4:6], referring to the things which he was writing in this Epistle. However, before Timothy could lay these things before others, he first had to feed on them himself. He had to digest them, assimilate them, and allow them to saturate his inner being. Then he would be able to lay them before the brothers. Today we should follow Timothy's example and lay before the saints the things with which we have been nourished by the Lord through the ministry. How wonderful the church life would be if we all did this! However, if we turn from the ministry and seek to produce something different, we may give place to differing teachings. It was not Timothy's intention to teach anything different from what Paul taught. Rather, he would lay before the brothers what he had received from Paul.

In verse 6 Paul specifically speaks of "being nourished with the words of the faith and of the good teaching." The words of the faith are the words of the full gospel concerning God's New Testament economy....If you want to see the focal point of God's economy, study the books of Galatians, Ephesians, Philippians, and Colossians. We need to be nourished with the words of the faith, God's economy, found in these books.

According to verse 6, we should also be nourished with the good teaching which we have closely followed....[These] are the sweet words that contain and convey the riches of Christ to nourish, edify, and strengthen His believers....If we would teach others, we ourselves must first follow these words closely. Following them closely and being nourished with them, we shall then be able to feed others. (*Life-study of 1 Timothy,* pp. 70-73)

[First Peter 5:2-3 says, "Shepherd the flock of God among you, overseeing not under compulsion but willingly, according to God; not...as lording it over your allotments but by becoming patterns of the flock."] The church is God's flock and His possession;...it is not the possession of the elders. But God has allotted that church to the elders so that they may care for it and shepherd it....Even the elders themselves are a part of the church as the possession of God. (*Life-study of 1 Peter,* pp. 294-295)

Further Reading: Life-study of 1 Timothy, msgs. 5, 8

Enlightenment and inspiration: ______________________

____

____

____

Morning Nourishment

Acts 14:23 And when they had appointed elders for them in every church and had prayed with fastings, they committed them to the Lord into whom they had believed.

20:28 Take heed to yourselves and to all the flock, among whom the Holy Spirit has placed you as overseers to shepherd the church of God, which He obtained through His own blood.

1 Pet. 5:2 Shepherd the flock of God among you, overseeing not under compulsion but willingly, according to God; not by seeking gain through base means but eagerly.

The Spirit...establishes the elders in the churches. In Acts 20:28 Paul tells the elders of the church in Ephesus that the Holy Spirit had placed them among the flock as overseers. It was the apostles who had appointed the elders in every church (Acts 14:23). But here Paul, the leading one, who did the appointing says that the Holy Spirit had placed the elders as overseers to shepherd the church. This indicates that the Holy Spirit was one with the apostles in their appointing the elders and that the apostles had done this according to the leading of the Holy Spirit. This indicates that those who establish the elders in the churches must do so by following the indwelling Spirit in their spirit. In this way the arrangement of the eldership will be according to the leading and directing of the Holy Spirit. (*The Conclusion of the New Testament,* p. 1053)

Today's Reading

The existence of the churches is altogether due to the Holy Spirit, not due to the apostles. Although the apostles had appointed the elders, Paul says that this was the work of the Holy Spirit. This reveals that a church comes into existence only through the work of the Holy Spirit. In other words, the work of the apostles concerning the churches should be absolutely the work of the Holy Spirit. (*The Conclusion of the New Testament,* p. 1053)

The overseers in Acts 20:28 are the elders in verse 17. This proves that overseers and elders are synonymous terms denoting the same persons. To make an overseer a bishop of a district to rule over the elders of various localities in that district is grossly erroneous....The two titles refer to the same person: elder, denoting a person of maturity; overseer, denoting the function of an elder. It was Ignatius in the second century who taught that an overseer, a bishop, is higher than an elder. From this erroneous teaching came the hierarchy of bishops, archbishops, cardinals, and the pope. This teaching is also the source of the Episcopal system of ecclesiastical government. Both the hierarchy and the system are abominable in the sight of God.

In Acts 20:28 Paul speaks of the elders shepherding the flock. The main responsibility of the elders as overseers is not to rule over the flock but to shepherd the flock, to take all-inclusive tender care of the flock, the church of God. The elders are not placed in the church by the Holy Spirit as rulers but as shepherds. Shepherding the flock of God requires suffering for the Body of Christ as Christ did (Col. 1:24). This kind of shepherding with suffering will be rewarded with the unfading crown of glory (1 Pet. 5:4).

According to 1 Peter 5:1-3, the elders are not to lord it over the flock; that is, they are not to exercise lordship over the ruled (Matt. 20:25). Among the believers, besides Christ there should be no other lord; all should be servants, even slaves (Matt. 20:26-27; 23:10-11). The elders in the church can take only the leadership (not the lordship), which all the believers should honor and follow (1 Thes. 5:12; 1 Tim. 5:17). (*Life-study of Acts,* pp. 464-465)

The church is also the flock of God as God's possession, allotted to the elders for their care (1 Pet. 5:2-3). The local churches are the flock of God, His possession, His inheritance. He has allotted this inheritance to the elders, who are the trustees. God's possession is given to the elders for their care. (*Elders' Training, Book 11: The Eldership and the God-ordained Way (3),* p. 9)

Further Reading: Life-study of 1 Peter, msg. 32; *The Conclusion of the New Testament,* msg. 98

Enlightenment and inspiration: ______________

Morning Nourishment

Acts 2:42 And they continued steadfastly in the teaching and the fellowship of the apostles, in the breaking of bread and the prayers.

Titus 1:9 Holding to the faithful word, which is according to the teaching *of the apostles*, that he may be able both to exhort by the healthy teaching and to convict those who oppose.

The basic need for the building up of the Body of Christ is the apostles' teaching. We should have no particular teaching other than the teaching of the apostles, which is the teaching concerning Christ's person and redemptive work and concerning God's economy in faith (2 John 9-11; 1 Tim. 1:3-4; Jude 3; Titus 1:4).

If we do not have the apostles' teaching, what shall we do? This is like sailing without a compass. Without the apostles' teaching, we do not have the compass, and we do not know the direction to take. Thank the Lord that in His recovery, by His mercy, we do have the apostles' teaching. In the recovery He has given us this clear view. (*Elders' Training, Book 10: The Eldership and the God-ordained Way (2),* pp. 155-156)

Today's Reading

The apostles' teaching includes two main and crucial items. These items are revealed in Ephesians 4 and 1 Corinthians 14. Ephesians 4 speaks of one Body, one Spirit, one Lord, one faith, one baptism, and one God and Father (vv. 4-6). Many Christians would agree with these seven "ones." But many would not agree with the revelation in verses 11 through 16. These verses are also a part of the apostles' teaching as a continuation of the seven "ones." They tell us that all the gifted persons are for the perfecting of the saints....They go on to speak about the Body building itself up through the joints of supply and through each one part operating according to its measure. The application and practice of these verses cannot be seen in Christianity.

First Corinthians 14...reveals that the church meetings are meetings of mutuality, not meetings with one person speaking and the rest listening. All the attendants in the meeting should be speakers....Without the practice of Ephesians 4 and 1 Corinthians 14, how could the Body of Christ be built up? We must hold and practice the entire teaching of the apostles, without selection according to our preference.

The second need for the building up of the church is the eldership. The New Testament shows us that the building up of the Body of Christ, including all the local churches, involves the gifted persons—the apostles, prophets, evangelists, and shepherds and teachers (Eph. 4:11-12). These are the ones who give the apostles' teaching. The building up of the Body of Christ also involves the elders. It is the elders who put the apostles' teaching into practice. The apostles teach not only the saints in the churches but also the elders of the churches. Then the elders put the apostles' teaching into practice. The elders should never separate themselves from the apostles' teaching. For the building up of the church, we need the apostles' teaching and the eldership to practice it. We may have the apostles' teaching, but what about the proper eldership to carry it out?

The eldership is altogether a matter of shepherding. The elders should shepherd the church and take care of the church according to the apostles' teaching. The apostles' teaching in the New Testament shows us that Christ builds up His Body through all of His members....The gifted persons should not replace the other saints. They should teach and perfect the saints so that the saints can do the same thing that they do. Then all the members have a share in the building up of the Body. All the members should be put to use.

The God-ordained way which has been brought into the Lord's recovery in these recent years is prevailing to recover the functioning of the members of the Body of Christ. This way annuls the clergy-laity system. (*Elders' Training, Book 10: The Eldership and the God-ordained Way (2),* pp. 156-158)

Further Reading: Elders' Training, Book 10: The Eldership and the God-ordained Way (2), ch. 10; *Elders' Training, Book 3: The Way to Carry Out the Vision,* chs. 9-10

Enlightenment and inspiration: ______________

Morning Nourishment

Acts 20:28 Take heed to yourselves and to all the flock, among whom the Holy Spirit has placed you as overseers to shepherd the church of God, which He obtained through His own blood.

1 Cor. 12:31 ...And moreover I show to you a most excellent way.

13:7-8 [Love] covers all things, believes all things, hopes all things, endures all things. Love never falls *away*. But whether prophecies, they will be rendered useless; or tongues, they will cease; or knowledge, it will be rendered useless.

13 Now there abide faith, hope, love, these three; and the greatest of these is love.

8:1 ...Knowledge puffs up, but love builds up.

The church, being the object of God's love, was obtained, that is, redeemed, by God with His own blood (Acts 20:28). The blood shed by Jesus on the cross was God's own blood. God shed His own blood to pay the cost for the church in order to redeem it. The church became and still is the object of God's love. God's love needs an object. The wife is the object of the husband's love. In the Bible the romance between male and female is used to illustrate God's divine romance. The church is the female in this romance, that is, the object of the divine love.

The church, as both the Body and the bride of Christ, is the object of Christ's love (Eph. 5:2, 25-29)....The church is the Body of Christ. As His Body, the church becomes His counterpart, His bride. (*Elders' Training, Book 11: The Eldership and the God-ordained Way (3)*, pp. 9-10)

Today's Reading

In Acts 20:28 Paul says that the church of God has been obtained "through His own blood." This indicates the precious love of God for the church and the preciousness, the exceeding worth of the church in the eyes of God. Here the apostle...[touches] the value of the church as a treasure to God, a treasure which He acquired with His own precious blood. Paul expected that the elders as overseers would also treasure the church as God did.

Both the Holy Spirit and God's own blood are divine provisions for the church He treasures. The Holy Spirit denotes God's person, and His own blood, God's work. God's redemptive work acquired the church; now God's person, the all-inclusive life-giving Spirit (1 Cor. 15:45), cares for the church through the overseers.

[In Acts 20:28], in His charge to the elders of the church in Ephesus, Paul speaks both of the Holy Spirit and of God's own blood in order to indicate his feeling concerning the preciousness of the church. According to Paul's understanding, the church is altogether precious. The church is under the care of the Holy Spirit, and the church has been bought by God with His own blood. Hence, the church is a treasure in the sight of God. Paul treasured the church even as God does.

According to Paul's word in verse 28, the elders should consider the church very precious, regarding it as a treasure in the sight of God. The elders, in shepherding the church, should have the same feeling about the church that God has. (*Life-study of Acts,* pp. 465, 473-474)

The elders need to have a vision concerning the church (Matt. 16:16-18; Eph. 5:32). They need a vision to see all the foregoing items.

The elders also need to love the church as the flock of God (Acts 20:29). The church is God's flock, and the elders are those appointed by God to care for the flock. As such, the elders need to love the church. We should love the church as a mother loves her own children (1 Thes. 2:7). In taking care of a church we should never take the way of legality. If we take the legal way, we will bring trouble to ourselves. Love is the only way that can build up the church. (*Elders' Training, Book 11: The Eldership and the God-ordained Way (3),* pp. 11-12)

Further Reading: Elders' Training, Book 11: The Eldership and the God-ordained Way (3), ch. 1; *Life-study of Acts,* msg. 54

Enlightenment and inspiration: ____________________

____

____

____

Morning Nourishment

Acts 20:29-30 **I know that after my departure fierce wolves will come in among you, not sparing the flock. And from among you yourselves men will rise up, speaking perverted things to draw away the disciples after them.**

Rom. 16:17 **Now I exhort you, brothers, to mark those who make divisions and causes of stumbling contrary to the teaching which you have learned, and turn away from them.**

[In Acts 20:29] Paul indicates that wolves will come in from the outside to damage the flock, the church of God. In verse 29, Paul did not care for his own life, but he was very much concerned for the future of the church, which was a treasure to him as well as to God.

In verse 30,...the perverted ones among the believers in the church are always used by the devil, who hates the church, to draw the sheep away to form another "flock."

During our many years in the church life, we have experienced both the wolves and the perverted ones. The wolves come from outside the church, and the perverted ones rise up from inside the church. (*Life-study of Acts,* p. 475)

Today's Reading

When perverted ones rise up in the church, we may think that this indicates that we have not been careful in our work and that we have brought inside seed that has produced perverted ones....However, we may not have anything to do with the rising up of such ones. Consider Paul's work in Ephesus. The church in Ephesus was raised up, established, and carried on by Paul's ministry over a period of three years. To be sure, Paul did his work very carefully. Nevertheless, even Paul anticipated that certain ones would rise up to speak perverted things in order to draw away saints after themselves to form another "flock."

One of the Lord's parables in Matthew 13 speaks of the sowing of tares among the wheat (vv. 24-30, 36-43)....Although I do not know where the tares come from, I know that wherever the "wheat" is, there the "tares" will be also. This indicates that where the real believers are, there false believers will also be. This is unavoidable. It was unavoidable in Paul's work, and it will be unavoidable in our work today.

After working in Ephesus for three years, Paul warned the elders of the church there that wolves would come in among them and that certain ones would rise up to speak perverted things. We have seen this take place both in the Far East and the West. We should not expect that there will be wheat without tares. It is possible that in any local church certain perverted ones may rise up. ...We need to receive Paul's word. Although he did not know who the perverted ones would be, he predicted their rising up.

According to Paul's word in Acts 20:30, the purpose of the perverted ones is to draw away the disciples after themselves. Their intention is to draw away the saints to form another "flock." We have observed this over the years. We have seen that the intention of the perverted ones is to set apart a group of believers to become their following. Therefore, we should take heed to Paul's word concerning wolves entering in from without and perverted ones rising up from within. (*Life-study of Acts,* pp. 475-477)

Throughout the centuries there have been these two classes of negative people. Paul likened one class to wolves and the other class to perverted persons who would rise up from within the church to speak perverted things with the purpose of drawing away disciples after themselves. These two classes of people were there at Paul's time and they are still here today....Romans 16:17 tells us to keep a watchful eye on those who make divisions and causes of falling. This word by Paul was not just an admonishing word but a prediction, telling us what would happen. Within a short time, this word transpired at Ephesus (2 Tim. 1:15). (*Talks concerning the Church Services, Part One,* p. 21)

Further Reading: Life-study of Matthew, msg. 37; *Life-study of 2 Timothy,* msgs. 2, 4

Enlightenment and inspiration: ______________

____

____

____

Hymns, #1229

1 The church is Christ's deep longing
And His good pleasure too.
His every word and action
Is made with her in view.
His heart's love is established,
And nought can Him deter;
Before the earth's foundation
His thoughts were filled with her.

2 The eve of all creation
He mused on His delight,
And pondered every feature,
Well-pleasing in His sight.
Creation sprang to being,
But deep in Him did hide
A heart of depth unfathomed
Fixed on a glorious Bride.

3 And thus His will was 'stablished
His counterpart to gain:
This blessed, firm intention,
Eternally the same.
Though sin should e'en beguile man,
Then mock his helpless state,
He never could forsake her,
His yearning ne'er abate.

4 Then mercy richly flourished,
And love was, oh, so vast,
As graciously He sought her
With wisdom unsurpassed.
The love He gave to win her
God only comprehends!
His life laid down, an offering
Whose fragrance yet ascends.

5 And now in resurrection
To her He draws most near,
And with untold affection
In glory does appear.
As she beholds her Bridegroom,
His glory floods her heart,
'Til she, His Bride, is raptured,
His longed-for counterpart.

Composition for prophecy with main point and sub-points:

The Elders Being Slaves to the Saints to Take Care of Them in Everything and in Every Way for the Dispensing of Christ into Them

Scripture Reading: 1 Pet. 5:1-6; 2:25; Heb. 13:17; Exo. 21:1-6; Mark 10:45

Day 1

I. To shepherd the flock of God is to watch over the souls of the saints, being one with the Lord as the Shepherd and Overseer of their souls in His care for the welfare of their inner being and in His exercising His oversight of their real person (1 Pet. 5:1-6; 2:25; Heb. 13:17):

A. For the sake of the flock, the elders must enjoy the Lord every day as grace and truth so that they may be dispensers of grace and truth (Eph. 3:2; 4:29; 1 Tim. 3:2b; 5:17; 2 Tim. 2:24-26; Titus 1:9).

B. For the sake of the flock, the elders need to buy the oil every day (Matt. 25:3-4, 9), to pay the price to gain more of the Spirit, by buying the truth of God's economy (Prov. 23:23), buying gold refined by fire that they may be rich toward God, buying white garments that they may be clothed with Christ by living out Christ, and buying eyesalve as the anointing Spirit to heal their blindness (Rev. 3:18).

C. For the sake of the flock, the elders need to be faithful and prudent slaves, taking care of the Lord's possessions and investing their spiritual gift by giving the food of the word of God, the full gospel of God's economy, to the sinners, the believers, and the churches (Rom. 1:1; Matt. 24:45-47; 25:22-23).

Day 2

II. The elders should not lord it over God's flock, which is God's possession; the churches are God's possession, allotted to the elders as their portion entrusted to them by God for their care (1 Pet. 5:2-3):

A. To lord it over others is to exercise lordship over those who are ruled (Matt. 20:25); among the believers, we are all brothers, and only Christ is our Lord, our Master, and the Lord of the harvest (Matt. 23:8, 10; Luke 10:2).

B. Nothing is more unsightly than a person who struggles to be an authority; it is the most ugly thing for a person to try to control others in an outward way.

C. Ambition to be an authority or to be a great one is something that belongs to the Gentiles; we should drive this kind of spirit from the church (Mark 10:42-43; Matt. 20:26-27; 23:10-11).

D. The elders in the church can only take the leadership (not the lordship) by becoming patterns of the flock, taking the lead to serve and care for the church that the believers may follow (1 Pet. 5:3; 1 Thes. 5:12-13; 1 Tim. 4:12; 5:17).

Day 3

E. We should not tell the saints where to live, what to do, or where to go without prayer to honor Christ as the Head and without fellowship to honor Christ as the Body:

1. Without the life of the Head, there is no Body, and without the authority of the Head, there is no oneness of the Body; we must allow the life of the Head to rule us so that the Body can become one (Col. 2:19; Eph. 4:1-4, 15-16).
2. Any decisions that you make by yourself for others are an insult to the Spirit; none of us should ever tell others where they should go; if we do not pray and have proper fellowship with others, we insult the Lord and usurp His position (cf. 2 Cor. 4:5).
3. Although the Lord has burdened us to go to the campuses, we should not turn this into a movement; everything must be brought into the presence of the Lord, and everyone should pray until he is clear about the Lord's leading (Acts 16:6-10).

4. Concerning any move you make in the Lord's recovery, you must go directly to the Lord Himself and pray; you must have the assurance that the Lord is sending you (Mark 1:35-38; 2 Cor. 2:12-14; Gal. 2:1-2a).
5. We also need to check whether the leading we have from the Lord corresponds to the feeling of the Body (Acts 13:1-4a; 21:4, 11).
6. If the leading ones, after much prayer, are truly burdened about a certain matter, through fellowship they should pass on their burden to the saints and ask the saints to pray; eventually, the saints will receive a personal leading from the Lord, and they may move accordingly; in this way no one will be individualistic or rebellious (cf. 1 John 1:3).
7. If you move to a place without prayer and fellowship, you will be shaken when tests, afflictions, and persecutions come; if you pray and fellowship, you will have the assurance that the Lord sent you there, and you will never regret your move no matter what the outward situation may be (2 Cor. 2:12-14; cf. 7:5-6).
8. We all need to pray earnestly that we would be kept in the Spirit and in the unique oneness of the Body; to be in the Spirit and in the unique oneness of the Body is to be kept in the Lord's recovery (Eph. 4:2-4).

Day 4

F. We need to be careful about directing or controlling the young saints related to their marriage (Matt. 19:5-6):
1. In the church life all we can do concerning the young saints' marriage is to minister life to them; we must help them to look to the Lord's leading, to learn how to walk in the Spirit, and help them not to indulge in lust or to have their own taste or choice (Gen. 2:21-24; 24:64-67; 49:31).

2. We should not try to conduct them into a marriage or match them; only the Lord knows who is a good match for another person; we do not know.
3. We do not control and, even the more, we do not conduct or indicate what brother or sister might be best for them; if we leave this matter to the Lord and pray for the ones concerned, we will save the church much trouble.
4. On the one hand, we should not interfere with them; on the other hand, we have to help them in morality, in life, in human living, in taking care of the future, in their relationship with their parents, and even in praying and seeking the Lord concerning the one whom they marry not being their choice.

Day 5 **III. All of the elders should be willing to be a slave to the saints; the elders should gird themselves with humility to serve the saints, humbling themselves under the saints (1 Pet. 5:1, 5-6; 2 Cor. 4:5; Matt. 20:26-27):**

A. The slave in Exodus 21:1-6 is a type of Christ, who emptied Himself, took the form of a slave, humbled Himself, and sacrificed Himself to serve God and His people; the Lord came not to be served but to serve (Phil. 2:5-8; Matt. 20:28; Mark 10:45; Eph. 5:2, 25):
   1. Love is the motive and prerequisite for a slave's continued service; the Lord Jesus loved the Father (His Master—John 14:31), the church (His wife—Eph. 5:25), and all the believers (His children—Gal. 2:20b; Eph. 5:2).
   2. All who believe in Christ, belong to Him, and have His serving life should take Him as their pattern (Matt. 20:26-28; Rom. 1:1; Phil. 2:5-8).

3. We have Christ's life of sacrifice, and His constraining love motivates us to consecrate ourselves to Him to be His slaves, loving God, the church, and God's people (Exo. 21:5; 2 Cor. 5:14; Rom. 1:1; cf. Gal. 6:17).
4. We need the spirit of a slave, the love of a slave, the obedience of a slave, and the life of a slave; only those who are willing to be slaves can remain permanently in the church life (5:13-16; cf. Phil. 2:17; Judg. 9:13).
5. A slave should take the position of doing nothing on his own but acting only according to the word of his master and should have his ear open to hear the voice of his master (Exo. 21:6; John 5:30; Psa. 40:6; Isa. 50:4-5; Luke 10:38-42).

B. We should lay down our human life, our soul-life, for the brothers; the divine life *(zoe)* within us longs to love others and even to die for them (1 John 3:16):
1. Every elder should be a martyr, one who sacrifices his life for Christ; nothing is more noble than living a martyr's life and dying as a martyr for the Lord (1 Pet. 5:1; 4:19; Acts 4:19-20; 8:1; John 21:18-19; Col. 1:24).
2. To be poor in spirit is to realize that we have nothing, know nothing, and are nothing; to be willing to be nothing is to lose our soul-life and is the real denial of the self on behalf of the brothers for the best enjoyment of Christ as the reality of the kingdom (Matt. 5:3; Gal. 6:3).
3. We are willing to be nobody and to exalt Christ, who is the only Somebody with the universal preeminence; we like to be nobodies because by being nobodies we are truly one, and Christ is all and in all (Col. 1:18b; 3:10-11).

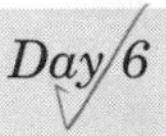
Day 6

IV. We need to take care of the saints in everything and in every way for the dispensing of Christ into them:

A. The elders must minister Christ to meet the need of all kinds of people, contacting and visiting them regularly and inviting them to their home for meals (1 Tim. 5:1-2; 2 Chron. 1:10; Col. 1:28-29; John 12:1-11; cf. Jude 12).

B. We must contact the saints and minister Christ to them as the sin-dealing life; the life of Christ is a life that deals with sin, a sin-dealing life (Lev. 10:17):

1. If we are going to minister Christ to a person who has been committing sins, we have to trust in the Lord that we may have the grace with the Spirit to soften his hardened heart (Rom. 2:4; Titus 3:3-4; Heb. 3:13).
2. We do not need to mention his weakness, fault, or sin, because the life of Christ ministered into him will heal him, killing the germs, destroying the problems, and building up a permanent, lasting oneness of the Spirit.
3. We have to do our best to recover a fallen saint; even if it would take eight months or a year to get one or two sinful saints recovered, this would be a great thing (Gal. 6:1-2; 1 John 5:16a).
4. This is to bear away the iniquity and solve the problems of the people of God; furthermore, this kind of ministry by the Spirit and in love will maintain the oneness of the Spirit in the church life (Col. 3:12-15).

Morning Nourishment

Heb. 13:17 Obey the ones leading you and submit to *them*, for they watch over your souls as those who will render an account, that they may do this with joy and not groaning; for this would be unprofitable to you.

1 Pet. 5:2 Shepherd the flock of God among you, overseeing not under compulsion but willingly, according to God; not by seeking gain through base means but eagerly.

To shepherd the flock of God [1 Pet. 5:2] requires suffering for the Body of Christ, as Christ suffered (Col. 1:24). This will be rewarded with the unfading crown of glory (1 Pet. 5:4).

According to 1 Peter 5:2, elders are not rulers; they are shepherds. Sometimes a shepherd may have to rule the flock, but that is not the ruling of a king. It is a ruling of someone who cares for the flock. Shepherding is a proper care exercised over the flock. The flock needs to be cared for, protected, and led in the right direction. They need to be brought to a place where they can eat and drink. This is shepherding.

In 5:2 Peter does not tell the elders to shepherd their own flock. He charges them to shepherd the flock of God. The flock is not the elders' possession, but God's possession. In a sense, the elders are employed by God to shepherd His flock. (*Life-study of 1 Peter*, p. 291)

Today's Reading

The elders should not regard the church in which they are taking the lead as belonging to them. In the New Testament...the church is called the church of Christ, the church of God, and the church of the saints (Rom. 16:16; 1 Cor. 1:2; 14:33). But the church is not the church of the apostles or the church of the elders. The church definitely does not belong either to the apostles or to the elders....However, it is possible for an apostle to think since a certain church has been raised up through his ministry, that that church belongs to him. Likewise, the elders may think, because they are taking the lead in the church, that the church is theirs. But Peter makes it clear that the elders are to shepherd the flock of God, not their own flock.

The word "overseeing" in 1 Peter 5:2 means taking the oversight, looking diligently to be aware of the situation. Years ago I thought that the overseeing was to observe who is wrong and who is right, who is doing well and who is doing poorly. Later I came to realize that to oversee is mainly a matter of overseeing the need. For example, when a shepherd is overseeing the flock,...he is concerned with the need of the flock. His oversight is related to protecting the flock, leading the flock, and feeding the flock. The shepherd exercises oversight in order to supply the flock with whatever is needed.

The elders must realize that the Lord has not appointed them to be rulers exercising authority over others. Ruling over others is something ugly and base. The elders should never rule over anyone. In the Gospel of Matthew the Lord Jesus said that He is the only Lord and Master and we all are brothers (Matt. 23:8,10). This means that the elders, the leading ones, are also no more than brothers.

In verse 3 Peter goes on to say, "Nor as lording it over your allotments but by becoming patterns of the flock." To lord it over others is to exercise lordship over those who are ruled (Matt. 20:25). Among the believers, besides Christ there should be no lord....All the elders should be slaves of the saints. It is not adequate for the elders even to be servants; they must be slaves....Peter heard the Lord Jesus say that those who desire to become great must be slaves. Elders should regard themselves as slaves, and the brothers and sisters as their masters.

Instead of lording it over the allotments, the elders should become patterns of the flock. This means that they take the lead to serve and care for the church so that the believers may follow. (*Life-study of 1 Peter,* pp. 292-295)

Further Reading: Life-study of 1 Peter, msg. 32; *The Vital Groups,* msgs. 6-7; *The Way to Practice the Lord's Present Move,* chs. 8-9; *The God-man Living,* msg. 2; *Authority and Submission,* ch. 18

Enlightenment and inspiration: ______________________

____

____

____

Morning Nourishment

Luke 10:2 ...He said to them, The harvest is great, but the workers few; therefore, beseech the Lord of the harvest that He would thrust out workers into His harvest.

Acts 15:28 For it seemed good to the Holy Spirit and to us...

We must learn from the experience of the apostles and elders in Acts 15 never to make decisions on our own....At the time of the Acts, Peter, Paul, and the other apostles were not qualified by themselves to make decisions or give instructions. Then what about us? We must honor the Lord. We are not the Lord or the Master, and we are not the Lord of the harvest. Only the Lord Jesus is the Lord of the harvest. He is the Master, and we must honor Him by not making decisions in ourselves. Suppose I am your servant, and you are my master. Suppose that without you I make certain decisions and then give instructions to others, making decisions for them as well. This would be a great insult to you. You are the master, but who am I? Nevertheless, we have all transgressed in this respect in the past, for a lot of decisions have been made among us. Some decisions were made by individuals and others by groups. In certain cases some even made decisions for others. But where is the Lord? When we make decisions in this way, it seems that there is no Lord among us. It seems that we do not have the Spirit, but only ourselves to depend on. (*The Spirit and the Body,* pp. 5-6)

Today's Reading

Although the Lord has burdened us to go to the campuses, we should not turn this into a movement. Any decisions that you make by yourself for others are an insult to the Spirit....None of us should ever tell others where they should go. What an insult this is to the Lord!...You need to help the others to contact the Lord. Young brothers and sisters, you need to pray. Yes, we are burdened and led of the Lord to work on the campuses. But the young people must bring this matter to the Lord, pray, and offer themselves to the Lord once again, saying, "Lord, I want to go on with You. Lord, where do You want me to go?" Everyone must pray until he is clear about the Lord's leading. Do not expect others to instruct you where you should go. That is organization, religion. Every one of us, from the leaders to the least among us, must be brought into the presence of the Lord to contact Him. Yes, the Lord is moving to the campuses, but perhaps in His sovereignty He will not allow you to go. He may lead hundreds of others to go, but He may tell you to stay where you are. This will be a proof that what is taking place among us is not a movement, but absolutely a matter of the Lord's leading.

The tragic history of Christianity must not be repeated among us. We must not insult the Lord and offend Him by not caring for His leading. We do not agree with any manmade decision. Everyone in the Lord's recovery must go directly to the Lord and pray. If anyone asked me where he should go, I would give him just one word—pray. Pray until you are clear, and then go. Do not ask me or anyone else what you should do. None of us is the Lord. Only Jesus Christ is the Lord.... You must inquire of Him, "Lord, where should I go?" If you do not get the Lord's leading, do not go to others and ask them to tell you what you should do.

Concerning any move you make in the Lord's recovery, you must go directly to the Lord Himself and pray.... You must have the assurance that the Lord is sending you.... You must be able to say, "I am here because the Lord sent me here. He asked me to come to this place and He wanted me here." We all must be clear concerning the Lord's leading to this extent.

Now is the time for us to have a genuine turn before the Lord. You must say, "Lord, we don't want to offend You or insult You. We want to honor You by waiting on You for Your leading." This is the Lord's recovery, not a repetition of the pitiful history of Christianity. Do not take orders from anyone and do not give orders to anyone. Go to the Lord and pray. This is the proper way. (*The Spirit and the Body,* pp. 6-10)

Further Reading: The Spirit and the Body, msg. 1; *Authority and Submission,* chs. 1-2

Enlightenment and inspiration: ________________

Morning Nourishment

Acts 13:2-4 **And as they were ministering to the Lord and fasting, the Holy Spirit said, Set apart for Me now Barnabas and Saul for the work to which I have called them. Then, when they had fasted and prayed and laid their hands on *them*, they sent them away. They then, having been sent out by the Holy Spirit...**

Suppose the leading ones, after much prayer, are truly burdened about a certain matter. What they should do then is through fellowship pass on their burden to the saints and ask the saints to pray. Eventually, the saints will receive a personal leading from the Lord, and they may move accordingly. In this way no one will be individualistic or rebellious. This is why we have the Body. We have both the Spirit on the one hand and the Body on the other hand. The Spirit and the Body keep us in balance. You need to check whether or not the leading you have from the Lord corresponds to the feeling of the Body. We need to be balanced. (*The Spirit and the Body,* p. 10)

Today's Reading

When some hear about being balanced by the Body, they may think that this matter of balance will produce the same result as if the leading ones made the decision and told them where to go. It is possible that the outward result may be the same, but the inward nature is absolutely different. Suppose I am a leading one and make decisions for others....I then tell the others to what place they should move....To do this is to usurp the position of the Lord and to make myself the Lord. This is the greatest insult to the Lord. Instead of doing this, I should say, "Brothers, I feel burdened of the Lord to share with you that some of you may need to move to a certain city. I ask you to please pray thoroughly about this matter." Eventually, some may be burdened by the Lord and led of Him to go to that place. Others, however, may be burdened to go to a different place. After you have received a burden from the Lord, you need to take care of the Body. Thus, we take care of both sides, the side of the Spirit and the side of the Body.

You may wonder where the Body is in a practical way. The Body is in the fellowship, and this fellowship is in unity. It is not a partial fellowship or fellowship relating to a division or an opinion. No, it is the fellowship of the Body. Fellowship follows prayer. After you have had prayer and fellowship, then you will be clear regarding the Lord's leading.

Some may say, "The result is exactly the same as if there were no prayer or fellowship. It is the same as if someone gave me an order to go somewhere. If that is the case, then why should we pray and have fellowship?" We must pray and fellowship in order to honor the Lord. If we do not pray and have the proper fellowship with others, we insult the Lord and usurp His position. Furthermore, if you move to a place without prayer and fellowship, you will be shaken when the tests, afflictions, and persecutions come....However, if you pray and fellowship, you honor the Lord, and you will also have the assurance that it is the Lord who is leading you. Then after you move to a certain place,...you will be so assured that your being there is the Lord's will and leading that you will be ready to die there....Because you have been sent by the Lord, not by any man, you will have the authority to pray. I hope you can all see the difference between being sent by the Lord and being sent by man.

In the churches and with the saints we must care for two elements: the Spirit and the Body. We must ask, "Is this the Spirit?" and, "Is this for the Body, or does this cause division?" We must be certain that what we are doing is in the Spirit and that it takes care of the unity. We do not want to become a movement that cares nothing for the Spirit; neither do we want to be a repetition of the division and confusion of the Christianity that does not care for the unique unity. We look to the Lord for His mercy and grace that we may always care for the Spirit and the Body. The Body is expressed in a practical way in the unique unity....To be in the Spirit and in the unique oneness of the Body is to be kept in the Lord's recovery. (*The Spirit and the Body,* pp. 10-11, 14)

Further Reading: The Spirit and the Body, ch. 1

Enlightenment and inspiration: ______________

Morning Nourishment

Matt. 19:5-6 **And [He] said, "For this cause shall a man leave his father and his mother and shall be joined to his wife; and the two shall be one flesh."...Therefore what God has yoked together, let man not separate.**

We must always keep in mind that the real, actual, and prevailing function of the elders is to minister life, to feed people. Based upon this principle, I would like to pass on a very crucial and practical point to you. The elders should stay away from the saints' practical life matters such as marriage. The saints may come to you, especially the young ones, to get your help concerning their marriage, their choice in marriage, and even concerning their dating. I do not mean that we older ones should not help them, but there is a great temptation in helping them in these kinds of things. Eventually, we could fall into directing them or even somewhat controlling them. This is very dangerous.

When young saints came to me forty-five years ago, I always had some principles and regulations to pass on to them. I always had the instructions ready, and I fully trusted that my principles were really right and prevailing....[But] today if anyone comes to me to talk about their marriage or about their choice in marriage, I have no burden and no interest. I have learned not to give the young saints advice concerning whom they will marry. I even told my closest relatives to just trust in the Lord concerning their marriage. Only the Lord knows who is a good match for another person. We do not know. (*Elders' Training, Book 4: Other Crucial Matters concerning the Practice of the Lord's Recovery,* p. 108)

Today's Reading

In the church life all we can do concerning the young people's marriage is to minister life to them. We must help them to look to the Lord's leading, to learn how to walk in the Spirit, and we should also help them not to indulge in lust or to have their own taste or choice. This is all we can do. We should not try to conduct them into a marriage or match them.

There should not be any kind of controlling among us

concerning the young saints' marriage....There is a temptation that the older ones among us would think that they could help the young ones. This, however, is the human hand, not the Lord's hand.

The matter of marriage is very complicated and is most perplexing. We should try to be very objective and try to render life to the young ones. Never try to bring two people together without any caution. This is dangerous. Some of you may feel that you did this once and that you were very successful. You may have been successful in one marriage, but do not take that as an encouragement. There is no need for us to touch this matter in a natural way. We should leave this matter to the Lord and pray for the ones concerned. We should render as much life as we can to help them and never indicate who is their best match. We do not control, and even the more, we do not conduct or indicate what brother or sister might be best for them. If we leave this matter to the Lord, we will save the church much trouble.

On the other hand, when the elders realize that some young saints are dating in an improper way, they must render them some help....It is altogether not safe for a young brother to be with a young sister in a loose way. Also, the elders should help them to consider their future. They should consider the matter of not getting engaged too quickly before marriage. They also must consider things regarding their family, their parents, their job, their financial situation, and other responsibilities. This is a real help in their human life....We should help them to learn how to pray about their marriage and how to look to the Lord to restrict their indulgence and lust. We have to help them in morality, in human life, in spirituality, and in the Lord's way. They are young in the Lord and need this kind of help....They should be helped to leave this matter to the Lord. As elders, we should do this because we are shepherding the flock. (*Elders' Training, Book 4: Other Crucial Matters concerning the Practice of the Lord's Recovery,* pp. 109-110)

Further Reading: Elders' Training, Book 4: Other Crucial Matters concerning the Practice of the Lord's Recovery, ch. 9

Enlightenment and inspiration: ______________

____

____

____

Morning Nourishment

Exo. 21:5-6 **But if the servant plainly says, I love my master, my wife, and my children; I will not go out free; then his master shall bring him to God and shall bring him to the door or to the doorpost, and his master shall bore his ear through with an awl; and he shall serve him forever.**

The slave in [Exodus 21:1-6 typifies] Christ. The Lord Jesus lived on earth as a slave. Thus, as the standard of the highest human living, the Lord in His living fulfilled the requirement of the first ordinance of the law concerning our relationship with others.

According to Exodus 21, a slave who loved his master and wanted to remain in his service was brought to the doorpost, and his ear was bored through with an awl (vv. 5-6). This indicates that a slave's ear was to be opened to hear the voice of his master.

In John 14:31 the Lord Jesus said, "But this is so that the world may know that I love the Father, and as the Father commanded Me, so I do." Because the Lord Jesus loved God the Father, He kept the Father's word not only as a Son, but especially as a slave. He listened to God and did God's will by keeping His word. It was the will of God that the Lord Jesus die on the cross to redeem God's chosen people. The Father gave this commandment to the Lord, and out of love for the Father the Lord obeyed Him as a slave and went to the cross. Thus, His death on the cross was an act of obedience. Paul says that Christ became "obedient even unto death, and that the death of a cross" (Phil. 2:8). Out of obedience to God, Christ died in a shameful manner. He died the death of a criminal, of a malefactor, executed by crucifixion according to the way of the Romans. Only a slave would be willing to die in this way. (*Life-study of Exodus,* pp. 806-808)

Today's Reading

As One who Himself became a slave, the Lord Jesus taught His disciples, at the very time they were striving to be first, to take the position of a slave. He said to them, "Whoever wants to be first among you shall be your slave; just as the Son of Man did not come to be served, but to serve and to give His life as a ransom for many" (Matt. 20:27-28).

According to Exodus 21:2, a Hebrew slave was to be set free after serving his master six years. If he obtained a wife and children during his years as a slave, he was to leave them as the property of his master and "go out by himself" (v. 4). However, the slave might plainly say, "I love my master, my wife, and my children; I will not go out free" (v. 5). Here we see that continuing as a slave is not a legal requirement; it is a matter of love. Because the slave loved his master, his wife, and his children, he did not want to go out free. Instead, he would serve his master forever. Love is the basis of his continued service.

As those who believe in Christ, we all must be His slaves. We should say, "O Lord, I love You. Even if I have the freedom to go out, I do not want to leave. I love You, I love Your church, and I love Your children."...The New Testament as well as the Old indicates that God's people need the spirit of a slave.

The elders in the churches need to realize that if they are not willing to be slaves, they cannot be proper elders. Every elder must be a slave. This was the reason the Lord Jesus taught His disciples not to seek to be above others, but instead to place themselves lower than others and be their slaves. In the church life there is no rank. We are all brothers, and we all must serve as slaves.

Only those who are willing to be slaves can remain permanently in the church life. No matter how I may be treated by the saints, I have no choice but to remain in the church life. The church is the home of my Father and of all His children. I am simply one of His slaves, loving Him, loving the church, and loving His children....If we have the spirit of a slave and the love of a slave, it will be easy for us to obey. Love is always followed by obedience.

As those who believe in Christ, belong to Him, and have His life of sacrifice, we also must be slaves loving God, the church, and God's people. With such a love as our motivation, we need to be slaves sacrificing and serving. (*Life-study of Exodus,* pp. 809-812)

Further Reading: Life-study of Exodus, msg. 68; *Consecration*

Enlightenment and inspiration: ______________

Morning Nourishment

Col. 1:28 Whom we announce, admonishing every man and teaching every man in all wisdom that we may present every man full-grown in Christ.

Lev. 10:17 ...For [the sin offering] is most holy, and He gave it to you to bear the iniquity of the assembly, to make expiation for them before Jehovah.

In their contact with people, the elders should minister Christ to them to meet their need (Eph. 3:8; Col. 1:28). They should minister Christ to everyone—the stronger ones and the weaker ones, the overcoming ones and the defeated ones, those with a good background and those with a bad background. We must be the same toward every person. It is easy for us to minister life to a brother we regard highly, but we may be cold and indifferent to another kind of brother. To behave in this way is to lose the opportunity to minister Christ to this brother. In the matter of ministering Christ to others, we may still have our own choice and preference. We may be willing to contact a brother like Timothy, but we may not take the time to help a brother like Demas, who loved the world and forsook Paul (2 Tim. 4:10). We may welcome Timothy but despise and reject Demas because Demas had a failure.

We must change our way of contacting people, staying away from catching or condemning people and learning to minister Christ to every kind of person. Eventually, people will be gained by the Lord through our contact. (*Elders' Training, Book 11: The Eldership and the God-ordained Way (3),* pp. 41-43)

Today's Reading

If you know that someone has committed some sins, you have to pray for him and learn to minister Christ as the sin-dealing life to him that he may deal with his sins. The life of Christ is a life that deals with sin, a sin-dealing life. Firstly, you yourself must be dealt with by enjoying Christ's sin-dealing life. Then you must minister such a Christ as the sin-dealing life to others. The book of Leviticus tells us that the priests were to eat the sin offering in the holy place that they might "bear the iniquity of the assembly, to make expiation for them before Jehovah" (10:17). As you are enjoying Christ as the sin-dealing life, you must have the capacity to bear the iniquity of God's people. You must learn to minister Christ to the dear ones who are in sin.

A person who sins usually has his heart hardened (Heb. 3:13). If you are going to minister Christ to him, you have to trust in the Lord that you may have the grace with the Spirit to soften his hardened heart. You have to soften his heart and warm up his heart. Then the very Christ as life will be actually, really, and richly ministered to him, and this life, which is the Spirit, will work within him. You do not need to mention his fault because the life that gets into him as the life supply will do a lot. If a person has a certain physical sickness, you do not need to mention his disease. If you minister the proper medication to this sick man, he will get well....This is...to bear the iniquity of the people of God. This is the way to get rid of the sins among some saints.

The work to recover the sinful saints takes time. It cannot be quick. You have to be patient. Even if it took eight months or a year to get one or two sinful saints recovered, that would be a great thing. Galatians 6:1 says that when a brother is overtaken in some offense, those who are spiritual should restore him. We have to do our best to recover a fallen saint. Out of one hundred saints meeting together, maybe two or three are living in a sinful situation. Since you are enjoying Christ, you can pick up the burden to take care of one of them. Another brother may have a burden for the same person. Then you and he can fellowship about this one saint and work together to help him. If you two can work together for half a year to get this sinful brother recovered, this is a great, great help to the church life. This kind of ministry is the element for us to maintain the oneness of the Spirit in the church life. (*A Timely Word,* pp. 13-14)

Further Reading: Elders' Training, Book 11: The Eldership and the God-ordained Way (3), ch. 5; *A Timely Word,* ch. 1; *The Exercise of the Kingdom for the Building of the Church,* ch. 7

Enlightenment and inspiration: ______________

Hymns, #398

1 O to be like Thee! blessed Redeemer;
This is my constant longing and prayer;
Gladly I'll forfeit all of earth's treasures,
Jesus, Thy perfect likeness to wear.

O to be like Thee! O to be like Thee!
Blessed Redeemer, pure as Thou art;
Come in Thy sweetness, come in Thy fullness;
Stamp Thine own image deep on my heart.

2 O to be like Thee! full of compassion,
Loving, forgiving, tender and kind,
Helping the helpless, cheering the fainting,
Seeking the wand'ring sinners to find.

3 O to be like Thee! lowly in spirit,
Holy and harmless, patient and brave;
Meekly enduring cruel reproaches,
Willing to suffer, others to save.

4 O to be like Thee! Lord, I am coming,
Now to receive th' anointing divine;
All that I am and have I am bringing;
Lord, from this moment all shall be Thine.

5 O to be like Thee! While I am pleading
Pour out Thy Spirit, fill with Thy love.
Make me a temple meet for Thy dwelling,
Fit for a life which Thou wouldst approve.

Composition for prophecy with main point and sub-points:

Being Fully Reconciled to God to Be Enlarged in Our Heart for Shepherding

Scripture Reading: 2 Cor. 5:20, 14-15; 6:11-13; John 21:15-17; Acts 20:28

Day 1

I. The ministry of reconciliation is to bring us back to God fully, thoroughly, completely, and entirely (2 Cor. 5:18):

A. The ministry of reconciliation is not merely to bring sinners back to God but, even the more, to bring believers absolutely into God.

B. Until we are wholly one with the Lord, being in Him and allowing Him to be in us absolutely, we will need the ministry of reconciliation.

C. Two steps are required for us to be fully reconciled to God:

1. In 2 Corinthians 5:19 it is the world that is reconciled to God, but in verse 20 it is the believers, who have already been reconciled to God and are to be reconciled further to God.
2. The first step of reconciliation is to reconcile sinners to God from sin (v. 19):
   a. For this purpose Christ died for our sins that they might be forgiven by God (1 Cor. 15:3; Luke 24:46-47; 1 John 2:12).
   b. This is the objective aspect of Christ's death; in this aspect He bore our sins upon Himself on the cross that they might be judged by God for us (1 Pet. 2:24; Isa. 53:11-12; Heb. 9:28; Col. 1:22; Rom. 8:3).

Day 2

3. The second step of reconciliation is to reconcile believers living in the natural life to God from the flesh (2 Cor. 5:20):
   a. For this purpose Christ died for us—the persons—that we might live to Him in the resurrection life (vv. 14-15).

b. This is the subjective aspect of Christ's death; in this aspect He was made sin for us to be judged and done away with by God that we might become the righteousness of God in Him (v. 21).

c. In the objective aspect of His death, Christ bore our sins; in the subjective aspect, He became sin (1 Pet. 2:24; Rom. 8:3; 2 Cor. 5:21).

d. Because we are still separated from God and because we are not fully one with God and altogether in harmony with Him, we need the second step of reconciliation.

Day 3

e. The subjective aspect of the death of Christ needs to be applied to our situation and to our natural life (Rom. 6:6; 8:13; Gal. 5:24; Matt. 16:24):

(1) In order that we may be reconciled to God in full, the Father exposes our natural life and unveils our real situation to us (1 John 1:5, 7):

(a) As a result, we condemn our natural being and apply the cross subjectively, and this application of the death of Christ crucifies our natural life.

(b) As our natural man is crossed out, we experience the second step of reconciliation; in this step the veil of our natural man is rent so that we may live in God's presence.

(2) Instead of taking place once for all, the second step of reconciliation is continuous.

4. By the two aspects of His death, Christ fully reconciles God's chosen people to God (Rom. 5:10; 2 Cor. 5:19-20).

Day 4

II. To be fully reconciled to God will cause us to be enlarged in our heart for shepherding (v. 20; 6:11-13; John 21:15-17; Acts 20:28):

A. How large our heart is depends on the degree of our reconciliation to God.

B. Narrowness of heart is a strong indication that we have been reconciled to God only partially and that the percentage of our salvation is quite low (2 Cor. 6:2; Rom. 5:10).

C. If we are able to forgive an offense and then forget it, that is a sign that we have become an enlarged person, a person with a large heart (Matt. 18:21-35; Eph. 4:32; Col. 3:13).

D. In order to be strict with ourselves and not with others, we need to be enlarged; those who are constricted are usually narrow as well, and thus they need to have their hearts enlarged (2 Cor. 6:12-13).

Day 5

E. "Judah and Israel were as numerous as the sand that is by the sea in multitude, eating and drinking and rejoicing…God gave Solomon wisdom and very much understanding and largeness of heart, even as the sand that is on the seashore" (1 Kings 4:20, 29):

1. Wisdom and largeness of heart are two aspects of one thing; the secret of wisdom is to have a large heart.
2. Those who are wise have a large heart, but those who have a narrow heart are foolish.
3. When a person is narrow and his heart is narrow, it is easy for him to be proud; pride is the expression of the narrowness of a person.

Day 6

F. We need to be impressed with the contrast between narrowness of heart and largeness of heart:

1. Narrowness of heart—not forgiving another party unless and until he repents; largeness of heart—having the loving and forgiving

heart of our Father God (Luke 15:20-24; 23:34a; Acts 7:59-60; Mark 11:25).

2. Narrowness of heart—caring for our own things; largeness of heart—caring for the things of Christ Jesus (Phil. 2:19-21).
3. Narrowness of heart—caring for individual spirituality; largeness of heart—caring for the church (1 Cor. 14:3-4, 12, 18-19).
4. Narrowness of heart—having a heart only for certain believers and churches; largeness of heart—having a heart for all believers and all churches, no matter what their condition may be (Phil. 1:8; 2:1-4; 2 Cor. 11:28).
5. Narrowness of heart—caring for our local church more than for the Body of Christ; largeness of heart—caring more for the Body of Christ than for our local church (Eph. 1:22-23).
6. Narrowness of heart—caring for our own work; largeness of heart—caring for the building up of the Body of Christ to consummate the New Jerusalem (4:16; Col. 2:19; Rev. 21:2).

Morning Nourishment

2 Cor. 5:14-15 For the love of Christ constrains us because we have judged this, that One died for all, therefore all died; and He died for all that those who live may no longer live to themselves but to Him who died for them and has been raised.

18 But all things are out from God, who has reconciled us to Himself through Christ and has given to us the ministry of reconciliation.

21 Him who did not know sin He made sin on our behalf that we might become the righteousness of God in Him.

What is the reconciliation ministered by Paul? I have read a number of books which refer to this subject, but none of them pointed out that the ministry of reconciliation is not merely to bring sinners back to God, but, even the more, to bring believers absolutely into God. Hence, it is not sufficient simply to be brought back to God; we must also be in Him. (*Life-study of 2 Corinthians*, p. 342)

Today's Reading

According to [2 Corinthians 5:21], we become the righteousness of God not merely through Christ, with Christ, or by Christ; we become the righteousness of God in Christ. From this verse we also see that we become not only righteous before God; we become the very righteousness of God. To be righteous is one thing, but to become righteousness is something else. For example, a certain thing may be golden, but it may not be pure gold. How wonderful that in Christ we may become the very righteousness of God!

Do you have the confidence to declare that you are in Christ? As genuine believers, we can testify that we are in Him. But are we in Christ in a practical way in our daily living? For example,...when you make a joke, do you have the assurance that you are in Him? You must admit that you are outside of Christ at such a time. There is no neutral ground: we are either in Christ or outside of Him. Because we are not always in Christ in a practical way, we need further reconciliation. We need to be reconciled back into Christ.

Suppose you are in a situation where you must wait in line for a long time. As you are waiting, you may feel not at all happy. In fact, you may be extremely bothered. Are you in Christ at that moment? No, you are outside of Christ. Where, then, are you? You are in yourself. At times your situation may be even worse, for you may be in the flesh, perhaps in your anger. Therefore, you need the ministry of reconciliation to bring you back into God once again.

I do not believe that many readers of 2 Corinthians 5 have the understanding that reconciliation is to be brought back into God. Was this your understanding of reconciliation in this chapter? Nevertheless, this is actually what Paul means by reconciliation.

The biblical understanding of reconciliation includes more than merely being brought back to God. It is to be brought back into Him. Therefore, according to the Bible, to bring others to God means to bring them into God and to make them absolutely one with Him. However, in much Christian teaching the matter of oneness with God is wrongly understood. According to the concept held by many Christians, to be one with God can be compared to a wife being one with her husband. In the case of a husband and wife, there is a kind of corporate oneness. But in the Bible to be one with God means to be mingled with Him. It is to be in God and to allow God to come into us. Biblical oneness with God is a oneness in which we enter into God and God enters into us. Therefore, the Lord Jesus said, "Abide in Me and I in you" (John 15:4). He did not say, "Abide *with* Me and I *with* you." What a shame that some Christians oppose this wonderful biblical concept of being one with God by being mingled with Him!

Until we are wholly one with the Lord, being in Him and allowing Him to be in us absolutely, we shall continue to need the ministry of reconciliation, the ministry with which Paul was commissioned. Paul was commissioned with the work of bringing the believers into God in a way that was absolute and practical. (*Life-study of 2 Corinthians,* pp. 342-344)

Further Reading: Life-study of 2 Corinthians, msgs. 38-39

Enlightenment and inspiration: ______________

Morning Nourishment

2 Cor. 5:18-20 But all things are out from God, who has reconciled us to Himself through Christ and has given to us the ministry of reconciliation; namely, that God in Christ was reconciling the world to Himself, not accounting their offenses to them, and has put in us the word of reconciliation. On behalf of Christ then we are ambassadors, as God entreats *you* through us; we beseech *you* on behalf of Christ, Be reconciled to God.

The books of 1 and 2 Corinthians show that the believers at Corinth, after being reconciled to God partially, still lived in the flesh, in the outward man. Between them and God there was the separating veil of the flesh, of the natural man. This veil corresponds to the veil inside the tabernacle, the veil that separated the Holy Place from the Holy of Holies, not to the veil at the entrance to the Holy Place. The Corinthian believers may have been in the Holy Place, but they were not in the Holy of Holies. This means they were still separated from the place where God is. Therefore, they had not been reconciled to God in full. (*Life-study of 2 Corinthians*, pp. 322-323)

Today's Reading

In 2 Corinthians 5:19 it is the world that is to be reconciled to God. In verse 20 it is the believers, those who have already been reconciled to God, who are to be reconciled to Him further. This clearly indicates that there are two steps for people to be fully reconciled to God. The first step is as sinners to be reconciled to God from sin. For this purpose Christ died for our sins (1 Cor. 15:3) that they may be forgiven by God. This is the objective aspect of Christ's death. In this aspect He bore our sins on the cross that God might judge them upon Him for us. The second step is as believers living in the natural life to be reconciled to God from the flesh. For this purpose Christ died for us—the persons—that we may live to Him in resurrection life (2 Cor. 5:14-15). This is the subjective aspect of Christ's death. In this aspect for us He was made sin to be judged and done away with by God that we may become the righteousness of God in Him. By the two aspects of His death He has fully reconciled God's chosen people to God.

These two steps of reconciliation are clearly portrayed by the two veils of the tabernacle. The first veil is called the screen (Exo. 26:36). A sinner was brought to God through the reconciliation of the atoning blood to enter into the Holy Place by passing this screen. This typifies the first step of reconciliation. The second veil (Exo. 26:31-35; Heb. 9:3) still separated him from God who is in the Holy of Holies. This veil needed to be rent that he might be brought to God in the Holy of Holies. This is the second step of reconciliation. The Corinthian believers had been reconciled to God, for they had passed through the first veil and had entered into the Holy Place. But they still lived in the flesh. They needed to pass the second veil, which has already been rent (Matt. 27:51; Heb. 10:20), to enter into the Holy of Holies to live with God in their spirit (1 Cor. 6:17). The goal of this Epistle is to bring them here that they may be persons in the spirit (1 Cor. 2:14), in the Holy of Holies. This is what the apostle means by saying, "Be reconciled to God."

[Most genuine Christians today] have been reconciled to God in part through the cross upon which Christ died....However, we have been reconciled to God only partly, halfway.

Although the Corinthians had been saved and reconciled to God halfway, they still lived in the flesh; that is, they lived in the soul, the outward man, the natural being. The veil of the flesh, of the natural man, still separated them from God. This means that their natural being was a separating veil. Therefore, they needed the second step of reconciliation. In 2 Corinthians 5 Paul was working to accomplish this second step. He was working on the Corinthians to cut the veil of the flesh asunder, to crucify their natural life, to consume their outward man. What the apostle Paul was doing in 1 and 2 Corinthians was to cleave the separating veil of the flesh so that the believers at Corinth could enter into the Holy of Holies. (*Life-study of 2 Corinthians*, pp. 323-324)

Further Reading: Life-study of 2 Corinthians, msgs. 36-37

Enlightenment and inspiration: ______________

Morning Nourishment

2 Cor. 5:20 On behalf of Christ then we are ambassadors, as God entreats *you* through us; we beseech *you* on behalf of Christ, Be reconciled to God.

6:1-2 And working together with *Him*, we also entreat you not to receive the grace of God in vain; for He says, "In an acceptable time I listened to you, and in the day of salvation I helped you." Behold, now is the well-acceptable time; behold, now is the day of salvation.

The blessings of God can be found in the Holy Place, but God Himself is in the Holy of Holies. In the Holy Place are the blessings of the Spirit, the lampstand, and the incense altar. But in the Holy Place there is not the direct presence of God. In order to have God Himself, we must be reconciled further and come into the Holy of Holies. We must take the second step of reconciliation to be brought into the presence of God. This is full reconciliation. This reconciliation brings us not only out of sin, but also out of the flesh, the natural man, the natural being. Then we are brought to God and become one with Him. (*Life-study of 2 Corinthians*, p. 325)

Today's Reading

I urge you not to cling to your old, limited concept of reconciliation....Take in this new, fuller understanding of reconciliation and see that to be reconciled is to be brought into God and that the ministry of reconciliation is the ministry of bringing others into God.

There were many problems among the believers at Corinth. All those problems were signs that those believers were not absolutely in God. In many particular matters they were not in God. Although they had been saved and born of God, they were not living in Him. For this reason, concerning many items in their daily living, they were outside of God. Therefore, Paul was burdened to bring them into God. This is to reconcile them to God.

Not only were the apostles commissioned with the work, the ministry, of reconciliation, but in bringing others into God they worked together with God. They knew that by themselves they could not bring anyone into God. They did not have this ability, this capacity. They needed to do this work with God.

In the past many of us said that we were working for the Lord. But when you were working for Him, did you have the sense that you were working with Him? There is an important difference between working for God and working with Him....Often we like to work for the Lord, but we do not want to work with Him. Our attitude may even be that the Lord should stay in heaven while we work for Him on earth. If we work in this way, we shall not be able to reconcile others into the Lord. Because we are not in the Lord ourselves in a practical way in our work, we cannot reconcile anyone else into the Lord. Only by working with the Lord can we reconcile others into Him.

To work together with God means that we are in Him. When we are in Him, we can bring others into Him. Only a person who is in God can bring others into God....Our closeness to God is the measure of the result of our work. If we are far away from God, we cannot bring others close to Him. The extent to which we can bring others to God and into God is always measured by where we are with respect to God. If we are those who are one with God, then we can bring others to the very place where we are. Therefore, if we want to bring others into the Lord, we must first be in Him ourselves. The more we are in Him, the more we can reconcile others into Him. May this matter be deeply impressed upon us!

In 2 Corinthians 6:2 Paul goes on to say, "For He says, 'In an acceptable time I listened to you, and in the day of salvation I helped you.' Behold, now is the well-acceptable time; behold, now is the day of salvation." The phrase "well-acceptable time" refers to the time of our being reconciled to God, in which He well-accepts us. Salvation in this verse, according to the context, refers to reconciliation. Reconciliation actually is full salvation. (*Life-study of 2 Corinthians*, pp. 344-346)

Further Reading: Life Lessons, lsn. 39; *Elders' Training, Book 6: The Crucial Points of the Truth in Paul's Epistles*, pp. 43-49

Enlightenment and inspiration: ____________________

____

____

____

Morning Nourishment

2 Cor. 6:11-13 **Our mouth is opened to you, Corinthians; our heart is enlarged. You are not constricted in us, but you are constricted in your inward parts. But for a recompense in kind, I speak as to children, you also be enlarged.**

The Corinthians had already received the grace of God. Their need was to allow this grace to work in them. If they allowed the grace of God to work in them, they would not receive God's grace in vain. This is to be reconciled to God in full and in every respect. Furthermore, this is to experience a present salvation. Today should be a day of further salvation, a day of progress in being reconciled to God through His grace. (*Life-study of 2 Corinthians*, p. 367)

Today's Reading

If we would be fully reconciled to God, fully saved, we need to be enlarged in our heart. Paul appealed to the Corinthians to be enlarged...(2 Cor. 6:12-13)....To be enlarged requires the aspects of the all-fitting life covered in 6:3-10. It requires the eighteen items beginning with "in": in endurance, in afflictions, in necessities, in distresses, in stripes, in imprisonments, in tumults, in labors, in watchings, in fastings, in pureness, in knowledge, in long-suffering, in kindness, in a holy spirit, in unfeigned love, in the word of truth, and in the power of God. It also requires the three pairs starting with "through": through the weapons of righteousness on the right and on the left, through glory and dishonor, through evil report and good report. Finally, it requires all the seven pairs beginning with "as": as deceivers and yet true, as unknown and yet well known, as dying and yet behold we live, as being disciplined and yet not being put to death, as made sorrowful yet always rejoicing, as poor yet enriching many, as having nothing and yet possessing all things. If we have all these characteristics of the all-fitting life, all the items with "in," "through," and "as," we have truly been enlarged.

We need to be straight and strict. However, we should be strict with ourselves, not with others. In order to be strict with ourselves and not with others, we need to be enlarged. Those who are very straight are usually narrow as well. They need to have their hearts enlarged.

When we become enlarged in our heart, we should not become loose. Rather, we should continue to be strict and straight concerning ourselves, but we should not apply this principle to others. If the Lord has done such a work in us, we have been enlarged.

I would ask you to consider once again all the matters covered by Paul in 6:3-10. If we have all these characteristics and qualifications, we shall have a large heart. We may be outwardly very small, but our heart will be like an ocean. But if we do not have these qualifications, we shall have a very small heart. We may be great in our own eyes, yet our heart may be extremely narrow. For example, our attitude may be that if a certain one makes a mistake, we should have nothing to do with him unless he repents. This is a sign of narrowness. It is also an indication that we are not able to reconcile others to God, for we ourselves have not been fully reconciled to Him. Our narrowness is a strong indication that we have been reconciled to God only partially and that the percentage of our salvation is quite low. How large our heart is depends on the degree of our reconciliation to God.

Both in your family life and in the church life you probably have been offended many times. Have you kept a record of all the offenses? Do you remember how your husband or wife offended you, or how you were offended by a certain elder? Do you remember all the offenses caused by the saints? We need to forgive and forget all offenses. We may forgive, but it may be harder for us to forget. This difficulty with forgiving and forgetting is caused by a heart that has not been adequately enlarged. Thus, we see once again that we need our hearts to be enlarged. To be fully reconciled and saved will cause us truly to be enlarged in our hearts. (*Life-study of 2 Corinthians,* pp. 367-370)

Further Reading: Life-study of 2 Corinthians, msgs. 41-42

Enlightenment and inspiration: ______________

____

____

____

Morning Nourishment

1 Kings 3:9-10 Give therefore to Your servant an understanding heart to judge Your people and to discern between good and evil. For who is able to judge this great people of Yours? And this word seemed good in the sight of the Lord, that Solomon had asked for this matter.

4:29 And God gave Solomon wisdom and very much understanding and largeness of heart, even as the sand that is on the seashore.

As an elder, a person must first have a heart that is large. Largeness is the first necessary condition of an elder's heart. In the Bible, there is one very good ruler, King Solomon....If we want to find a standard character on experiencing the cross, we have to go to David. But to find a standard character on managing God's people, we have to go to Solomon. Solomon was indeed competent at managing. We must remember, however, that King Solomon was competent at managing for two reasons: he had wisdom, and he had a large heart. Actually, these are two aspects of one thing. (*The Elders' Management of the Church,* pp. 38-39)

Today's Reading

[Solomon] wanted wisdom from God....The most necessary thing in management is wisdom. To have cleverness is not enough, because cleverness is common, whereas wisdom is extraordinary. Solomon deeply felt that for a young man to rule the myriads of God's people, he needed wisdom from God. That was why he sought for wisdom before God. Surprisingly, however, though he asked only for wisdom, God gave him, in addition to wisdom, also a large heart. First Kings 4:29 says...that largeness of heart is like the sand on the seashore.

At the time when God gave Solomon wisdom, He also gave him a large heart. We have to know that all wise ones have large hearts, and everyone with a narrow heart is a foolish person. If you want to be a foolish person,...simply make your heart small. ...If you enlarge your heart, you will become the wisest person. You cannot separate a large heart from wisdom and prudence.

A person who oversees God's people needs much wisdom, but the secret of wisdom is to have a large heart....You have no idea how much this matter affects those serving as elders. Many of your inaccurate judgments are caused by your narrow heart. On the surface it appears that you lack wisdom, but actually, the problem comes because your heart is narrow....If you would only enlarge your heart, immediately you would become a person of wisdom.

Therefore, brothers, learn to enlarge your heart in all things. ...Whether in learning the truth, in seeking to be spiritual, in contacting the brothers and sisters, in discerning others, or in managing affairs, we must learn to be large. Whenever we touch the affairs of the church and whenever we touch any spiritual matter, we have to learn to be large in our heart.

Once you visit another place, your heart will be enlarged. If circumstances allow, it would be even better to travel overseas. Once a man goes out for a visit, his heart will be enlarged....You must learn to enlarge your heart. It does not mean that to have a large heart is to be loose. You must still be strict with yourself, yet your heart toward others must be large.

Of course, the natural life can never learn this lesson. Often a natural man will make a pretension of trying to enlarge his heart. In order to enlarge our own heart, we need the Lord's abundant grace. Please remember that the ability to forgive others is a matter that has to do with the largeness of heart. The ability to bless the ones who curse us also has to do with a large heart. Your heart must be so large that whenever others offend you, you can forgive them as soon as they confess to you. Though others may persecute you and inflict harm on you, you can still love them. To be able to forgive others when they have offended you is something that has to do with a large heart. Oh, the wisdom that comes from a large heart is immeasurable! (*The Elders' Management of the Church,* pp. 39-43)

Further Reading: The Elders' Management of the Church, ch. 3; *The Collected Works of Watchman Nee,* vol. 37, ch. 13

Enlightenment and inspiration: ____________________

Morning Nourishment

2 Cor. 7:2-3 Make room for us; we have wronged no one, we have corrupted no one, we have taken advantage of no one. I do not say *this* to condemn *you*, for I have said before that you are in our hearts for *our* dying together and *our* living together.

8:1 Furthermore we make known to you, brothers, the grace of God which has been given in the churches of Macedonia.

4 With much entreaty they besought of us the grace and the fellowship of the ministry to the saints.

[In 2 Corinthians 7:2], when Paul says, "Make room for us," he is actually saying to the Corinthians, "Brothers, I want to enter into you and dwell in you. But you are narrow and have shut yourselves up. You don't have an enlarged heart to receive us. I love you, and I am concerned for you. This is why I urge you to open up and make room for us so that we may come into you and dwell in you."

In verse 3 Paul even says that the Corinthians were in the apostles' hearts to die together and live together. Here Paul seems to be saying, "I do not say this to condemn you, for I have already said that you are in our hearts. Since we have you in our hearts and our hearts are enlarged, we appeal to you to enlarge your hearts and make room for us. Corinthians, you are in our hearts to die together and live together." What deep, tender, intimate words! How deeply touching! (*Life-study of 2 Corinthians,* pp. 384-385)

Today's Reading

In his second Epistle, Paul first pointed out to the believers at Corinth that as ministers of the new covenant, the apostles had received the ministry to reconcile God's people fully back to Himself. Then in chapter six Paul carried on this ministry, doing a fine work to reconcile the distracted Corinthians back to God in full. After accomplishing such a work, he went on to fellowship with them that they should have a ministry to supply the needy saints.

The sequence in these chapters is important.…One chapter follows another like steps in a staircase.…Only after [Paul] had done an excellent work to reconcile the distracted saints back to God did he present them with the ministry of caring for the needy saints. Thus, we should not regard these chapters as separated and isolated. Apparently chapters eight and nine are on a different subject from chapters six and seven. Actually in Paul's thought all these chapters are connected.

Through Paul's reconciling work, the saints in Corinth were brought back to God, repented, and received more salvation. Then in 8:1 Paul says, "Furthermore, we make known to you, brothers, the grace of God which has been given in the churches of Macedonia." The word "furthermore" indicates that certain preparations have been made and that a particular atmosphere and condition exist for the writer to present something further. Thus, Paul goes on to speak of the grace of God bestowed upon the churches of Macedonia. His aim was that the Corinthian believers would participate in supplying the needy saints.

To have a ministry to needy saints we need to receive grace from God, from the apostles, and from the Lord Jesus Christ. Receiving this threefold grace, we can then supply others with a material gift in grace. Whatever we do in giving to others will not simply be a ministry of material things to take care of the needs of the saints, but will also be a supply of life to them. In this way, we communicate spiritual riches to those needy saints. This kind of giving is needed among us today.

Our material gifts should be spiritual, full of life, and able to edify the saints and build up the Body of Christ. This requires that when we give some material things to the Lord, we should have the assurance that we are doing it in spirit, with life, and for the building up of the church. This kind of giving is the issue, the result, of being fully reconciled to God. Only those who have been reconciled to God in full can have a ministry of material things that brings to the needy saints a supply of life for spiritual edification and for the building up of the Body of Christ. (*Life-study of 2 Corinthians*, pp. 399-400, 406-407)

Further Reading: Life-study of 2 Corinthians, msgs. 44, 46

Enlightenment and inspiration: ______________________
____
____
____

Hymns, #1214

1 Dig away, dig away, dig away,
Condemnation in my heart dig away!
Dig away, dig away, dig away,
Condemnation in my heart dig away!

All the guilt has to go
That His life may flow . . . Hallelujah!
Dig away, dig away, dig away,
Condemnation in my heart dig away!

2 Dig away, dig away, dig away,
All my vain imaginations dig away!
Dig away, dig away, dig away,
All my vain imaginations dig away!

All my dreams have to go
That His life may flow . . . Hallelujah!
Dig away, dig away, dig away,
All my vain imaginations dig away!

3 Dig away, dig away, dig away,
All my troublesome emotions dig away!
Dig away, dig away, dig away,
All my troublesome emotions dig away!

All self love has to go
That His life may flow . . . Hallelujah!
Dig away, dig away, dig away,
All my troublesome emotions dig away!

4 Dig away, dig away, dig away,
All resistance in my will dig away!
Dig away, dig away, dig away,
All resistance in my will dig away!

All self will has to go
That His life may flow . . . Hallelujah!
Dig away, dig away, dig away,
All resistance in my will dig away!

5 Dig away, dig away, dig away,
All self seeking in my heart dig away!
Dig away, dig away, dig away,
All self seeking in my heart dig away!

All my hopes have to go
That His life may flow . . . Hallelujah!
Dig away, dig away, dig away,
All self seeking in my heart dig away!

6 Life can flow, praise the Lord, life can flow!
From the fountain in my heart life can flow!
Life can flow, praise the Lord, life can flow!
From the fountain in my heart life can flow!

When my heart's wholly free,
Christ can flow through me . . . Hallelujah!
Life can flow, praise the Lord, life can flow!
From the fountain in my heart life can flow!

Composition for prophecy with main point and sub-points: ______________________________

The Urgent Need to Deal with Our Disposition

Scripture Reading: Matt. 16:24-26; Rom. 6:6; Gal. 2:20

Day 1

I. The most important matter that must be dealt with in our life with the Lord is our disposition:

A. The thing which most damages our usefulness in the Christian life, in the church life, and in the work is our living according to our disposition.

B. Our disposition has become our problem; it hinders us from growing in life and from being used by the Lord, and it has made trouble for us, causing us to suffer.

C. How useful we will be to the Lord or how much trouble we will make to the church depends upon how much our disposition is killed; therefore, dealing with the disposition is a crucial matter (2 Tim. 2:21).

D. The greatest hindrance to our usefulness is our disposition; disposition is the factor that spoils our usefulness in the hand of the Lord (Matt. 25:24-30):

1. Many dear saints have remained in the church, but their usefulness has been annulled by their disposition.
2. Many are useless and out of function mainly because of their disposition; if all the saints would deny their disposition, they would all be very useful.

E. Our disposition is the greatest problem for our growth in the divine life; the real enemy of our growth in the divine life is our disposition (cf. 2 Pet. 1:5-11).

F. We need the Lord to touch our disposition, and we need to deny it.

Day 2

II. We use the word *disposition* to help the saints to understand the soul-life, the self,

the "I," the old man, and naturalness (Matt. 16:24-26; Rom. 6:6; Gal. 2:20):

A. In our Christian experience, there is something within us called our disposition.

B. Our disposition is what we are in our makeup by birth; each of us has a particular and unique disposition.

C. Our disposition has been poisoned by the cunning, subtle serpent.

D. There are four terms mentioned in the New Testament which are closely related to the matter of disposition: the old man (Rom. 6:6), the "I" (Gal. 2:20), the soul-life (Matt. 16:25-26), and the self (v. 24):

1. Disposition is implied in the terms *mind, self,* and *soul-life;* disposition includes all of these elements.
2. The soul is the life of the self; disposition is closely related to both the self and the soul.
3. Practically speaking, to deny the self is simply to deny our disposition.

E. To deal with our disposition means to deal with our self, our old man, our soul-life, and the "I."

F. Since the disposition is implied in the "I," the old man, the soul, the self, and naturalness, our dealing with these things includes our dealing with our disposition.

Day 3 **III. Our dealing with sins, sin, the world, and the conscience are superficial dealings, but our dealing with our disposition is the deepest dealing (1 John 1:7; 2:15; Acts 24:16; Matt. 16:24-26):**

A. Although our disposition is something made by God, it still needs to be dealt with by God; this is according to the divine revelation, and it is also confirmed by our experience.

B. Our fallen disposition is close to the edge of the deep well of sin and mistakes; our mistakes and wrongdoings are closely related to our disposition.

C. Our disposition is the most difficult part of our being to deal with, and often there is a particular part of our disposition—a "burl"—that is the hardest thing to deal with:
   1. We must learn to take care of the "burl" in our makeup, our disposition.
   2. If we deal with this "burl," we will grow quickly and have a free way in our spiritual life without any hindrances to our growth in life, and we will also become more useful to the Lord.

D. Transformation is mainly with our disposition; in order to experience transformation, we need the breaking of our disposition because it is a great obstacle to God's dispensing of Himself into us and to His transforming work in us (Rom. 12:2).

E. The breaking of the outer man is the breaking of our disposition.

F. The best way to be dealt with is to hate our disposition; our disposition is the depth of the self, which must be denied (Matt. 16:24).

Day 4

IV. The solution to the problem of our disposition is the cross (Gal. 2:20):

A. Only the death of the cross can deal with our disposition.

B. In order to deal with our disposition, we must realize and remember that we have already been crucified and that, as a crucified person, we should remain under this realization day by day (Rom. 6:6; Gal. 2:20).

C. Because we have been crucified, we should not live according to our disposition, according to what we are naturally.

Day 5 & Day 6

V. The church life, fruit-bearing, and lamb-feeding are three matters that kill our natural disposition (John 15:4-7; 21:15-17):

A. If we are not useful in the Lord's hand for taking care of people, it is due to our raw, natural disposition:

1. Because of our disposition we have no interest in others, or if we do have such an interest, we are unable to minister life to others.
2. Our disposition is the cause for our not bearing fruit and not using our talent to care for people.
3. The burden to care for others requires us to deal with our disposition.

B. Receiving the believers because the Lord has received them requires us to deal much with our natural disposition (Rom. 14:1; 15:7).

C. A person who is capable and who is also against his or her disposition is the most useful person to the Lord (Matt. 25:14-23; 16:24).

D. What thc Lord needs is the exercise of our talent with the growth in life; in order to have this, the basic condition is to deal with our disposition.

Morning Nourishment

2 Pet. 1:5-8 And for this very reason also, adding all diligence, supply bountifully in your faith virtue; and in virtue, knowledge; and in knowledge, self-control; and in self-control, endurance; and in endurance, godliness; and in godliness, brotherly love; and in brotherly love, love. For these things, existing in you and abounding, constitute *you* neither idle nor unfruitful unto the full knowledge of our Lord Jesus Christ.

The ever present obstacle and frustration to our growth in our spiritual life is our opinion. Sometimes we do not express our opinion, but it is still there. Opinion is the expression of our disposition, and our disposition is the greatest problem for our growth in the divine life. In the Far East and in America, I have come to know a number of saints. They are lovely, they are very much for the Lord, and they mean business with the Lord. However, after many years, they have had little growth in life. Their unique problem is their opinion. (*The Experience and Growth in Life*, p. 144)

Today's Reading

Our disposition is our self. Every human being has a disposition. It is in us and it is us. Our disposition makes it hard for us to release our spirit....[When Brother Nee resumed his ministry in 1948], one of the first messages he gave was on the breaking of the outer man and the release of the spirit. From that time on, the center of Brother Nee's speaking was almost always on the breaking of the outer man. The breaking of the outer man is the breaking of our disposition. I am still learning the lesson of how to deal with my disposition. Brother Nee warned us that if we do not learn the lesson of the breaking of the outer man before we are fifty years old, we will have a difficult time in the church life. It is easier to deal with our disposition when we are young.

The thing which most damages our usefulness in the Christian life and church life is our living according to our disposition. I have been in the Lord's work for many years, and I have found that some brothers and sisters have a strong element in their disposition which hinders them from coordinating and cooperating with others. If certain brothers or sisters are assigned a certain work, no one else can be included with them to help in that work; they must do it exclusively. Such brothers or sisters are usually very capable, and they can also easily stir up trouble in the church life.

The Lord's work is a work of the Body and by the Body; therefore, coordination is desperately needed. The apostle Paul was very capable, but he also needed a number of others to help him and coordinate with him....Even the Lord Jesus Himself needed to coordinate with others. Actually, most of us do not like to work with others....If we are diligent persons, laboring all the time, we may not like others to work with us, because whatever they do interferes with what we are doing.

In our spiritual life, in our Christian life, in our church life, and in the Lord's work, we must learn to be people who are always opposing ourselves. As a person with a strong disposition, I can testify that I must constantly realize that my disposition is crucified. In the past, my confession was almost completely about my failure to live Christ. Today, very often my confession to the Lord is concerning my disposition. We must learn to live a life of opposing ourselves. To oppose ourselves is to oppose our disposition. Both the good and bad dispositions destroy our usefulness in the spiritual realm.

If all the saints, especially those who are being trained to serve the Lord full time, kill their disposition, everything will be very good. Otherwise, each trained one becomes a potential problem to the church. If we pick up the training and practice it with our ambition and capacity, trouble will be the result. If each trainee does not kill his or her disposition, each one is a problem and will be a problem. How useful you will be to the Lord or how much trouble you will make to the church depends upon how much your disposition is killed. Therefore, dealing with the disposition is a crucial matter. (*The Experience and Growth in Life,* pp. 144-145, 154-155, 157)

Further Reading: The Experience and Growth in Life, msg. 23; *The Breaking of the Outer Man and the Release of the Spirit,* ch. 2

Enlightenment and inspiration: ______________

Morning Nourishment

Matt. 16:24-26 Then Jesus said,...If anyone wants to come after Me, let him deny himself and take up his cross and follow Me. For whoever wants to save his soul-life shall lose it; but whoever loses his soul-life for My sake shall find it. For what shall a man be profited if he gains the whole world, but forfeits his soul-life? Or what shall a man give in exchange for his soul-life?

There are four terms mentioned in the New Testament which are closely related to the matter of disposition: the old man in Romans 6:6, the "I" in Galatians 2:20, the soul-life in Matthew 16:25-26, and the self in Matthew 16:24. In addition to these terms, according to our study and experiences of the spiritual things in the New Testament, we have also used the term *naturalness* in relation to the matter of disposition. The contents of these five terms all imply disposition. A person's disposition includes all of these items. (*The Experience and Growth in Life,* pp. 151-152)

Today's Reading

In our Christian experience, there is something within us called our disposition. This disposition is what we are in our makeup. Each of us has a particular and unique disposition. Inwardly in our disposition, we are quite different from one another.

Your disposition denotes what you are in your makeup by birth. Whatever you are by birth is your disposition. If you are slow, you were made slow by birth; being slow is your disposition. Likewise, if you are quick, quickness is your disposition. One may be silent or talkative; both are matters of inward disposition. Although our disposition is something made by God, yet it still needs to be dealt with by God. This seems to be contradictory—something given by God must be dealt with by God. However, this is very much according to the divine revelation, and it is also confirmed by our experience.

Our disposition is expressed in many forms. One type is that of the "hero." Brothers or sisters who have this type of disposition must do everything in an impressive, perfect, and complete way. If they are to speak, they must do it in an outstanding way, or they will not speak. They are also very strong and quick in doing things. Another type of disposition is that of the "non-hero." The "non-hero" does not do anything in a thorough or complete way.

Our disposition is what we are in our makeup by birth and... our character is the outward expression of our disposition. Disposition is what we are within, and character is what we express without. The reason we are silent or talkative is due to our disposition. At the start of our full-time training, some brothers and sisters spoke very often, but after some weeks passed, perhaps due to some word of correction regarding their speaking, they became very silent. Their outspokenness was related to their disposition, but their self-enforced silence is related to their character.

Slowness is a matter of disposition. We may do everything very slowly. If we are rebuked for our slowness, we may become offended and react by doing everything in an extremely fast manner. What we express in this change of our outward behavior is no longer our disposition but our character. Disposition by itself does not directly involve anything of sin. But once our disposition is expressed with a hurtful intention, that is sin. Thus, our disposition has little to do with sin directly, but our character has a great deal to do with sin.

While there are no verses in the New Testament which directly tell how to deal with the disposition, there are a number of verses which can be used. Since the disposition is implied in the "I," the old man, the soul, and the self, our dealing with these things includes our dealing with the disposition. In Galatians 2:20, the "I" has been crucified. This "I" implies the disposition. In the same way, when we deny the self (Matt. 16:24) and lose the soul-life (Matt. 16:25-26), the disposition is dealt with, because it is implied in these things. (*The Experience and Growth in Life,* pp. 136-137, 152-153)

Further Reading: The Experience and Growth in Life, msg. 21; *The Breaking of the Outer Man and the Release of the Spirit,* chs. 1, 3

Enlightenment and inspiration: ______________

Morning Nourishment

Luke 9:23 **...If anyone wants to come after Me, let him deny himself and take up his cross daily and follow Me.**

Matt. 19:25-26 **And when the disciples heard *this*, they were greatly astonished and said, Who then can be saved? And looking upon *them*, Jesus said to them, With men this is impossible, but with God all things are possible.**

Our dealings with sins, sin, the world, and the conscience are superficial dealings, but our dealing with the disposition is the deepest dealing. To deal with sins and sin is relatively easy, but to deal with our disposition and character is very difficult....Many times our disposition may not be right, but it is difficult to say that it is always sinful. Sometimes we are simply in our disposition and not in anything sinful. However, we must realize that our fallen disposition is close to the edge of the deep well of sin and mistakes. Thus, it is very easy for us to fall into this well.

Dealing with our disposition and character will safeguard us from making mistakes and committing sins. Our mistakes and wrongdoings are closely related to our disposition and character. (*The Experience and Growth in Life,* p. 138)

Today's Reading

Transformation deals mainly with our disposition, and renewal deals mainly with our character. Both transformation and renewal simply mean to deal with our disposition and character. A transformed person will not remain in his old disposition, and a renewed person will not remain in his old character or expression.

The divine dispensing always works to transform us, not only to correct or change us. To change is just to change yourself by your own effort. To transform indicates something divine, something of the Lord, which you do not have by your habits or birth. By the divine dispensing, a divine element is dispensed into you. This element works in you to transform you. If your countenance is pale, through eating, the element of the food will transform your pale color into a healthy color. This healthy color is a transformed color. Without the divine element dispensed into you, you could only have a change but not transformation.

In order for us to experience this transformation, there is the need of the breaking of our disposition and character because [they]...are the greatest obstacles to God's dispensing of Himself into us and to His transforming and renewing work on us.

According to my observation over many years, the real enemy of our growth in the divine life is our disposition. Our disposition is also the factor that spoils our usefulness in the hand of the Lord....I have learned that many saints eventually stopped growing in the divine life and could make no further progress...due to a particular, peculiar aspect of their disposition.

Our particular traits can be compared to the grain in a piece of wood. A carpenter prefers to use wood that has an even grain....A piece of wood may be of good quality, but if it has a knot or a burl, it cannot be sawed easily; it is not useful. The Christians who do not have any peculiarity, any peculiar traits, are the ones who grow the most and the fastest. Likewise, the brothers and sisters who are the most useful are the ones who do not have any peculiar traits. In the service, the ones who are the most useful are the ones who always reject and deny what they are.

By man's hand there is no way to remove the factor of the disposition, but in the Lord's hand there is a way. In Matthew 19:25 the disciples asked the Lord, "Who then can be saved?" The Lord replied, "With men this is impossible, but with God all things are possible" (Matt. 19:26). This word must have been fulfilled in Peter. In 2 Peter 1:5-11 Peter wrote concerning the development of what the Lord has given us by the growth in life unto the rich entrance into the eternal kingdom. Peter was able to write such a word because he had learned the spiritual lessons. The Lord broke through in him. It is impossible for us to break through the problem of our disposition, but it is possible for the Lord to do it. (*The Experience and Growth in Life,* pp. 139-140, 160-161, 163)

Further Reading: The Experience and Growth in Life, msg. 24; *The Exercise of the Kingdom for the Building of the Church,* ch. 3

Enlightenment and inspiration: ______________

Morning Nourishment

Rom. 6:6 Knowing this, that our old man has been crucified with *Him*...

Gal. 2:20 I am crucified with Christ; and *it is* no longer I *who* live, but *it is* Christ *who* lives in me; and the *life* which I now live in the flesh I live in faith, the *faith* of the Son of God, who loved me and gave Himself up for me.

In order to deal with our disposition, we must realize that we have been crucified (Gal. 2:20; Rom. 6:6). From morning to evening, throughout the entire day, we must remember that we are people who have already been crucified. Because we have been crucified,...we should not live, act, or walk according to what we are naturally. To live in such a way is simply to live according to our disposition. The way to deal with our disposition is to realize and remember that we are crucified persons and remain under that realization throughout the day. (*The Experience and Growth in Life,* pp. 153-154)

Today's Reading

Along with the realization that we are crucified, we have to oppose ourselves. To oppose ourselves is to oppose our disposition. If you realize that your disposition is to be quiet, as long as you remain quiet, you are simply living according to your disposition. But if you would oppose your quiet disposition, you must first realize that your natural person has been crucified and then remain under the killing of the cross. Then in the meetings you, opposing yourself, can exercise to speak something of the Lord to the saints.

The most fearful thing in the Lord's work is a capable person with ambition....One who is capable and without ambition is very useful in the Lord's work....The best example of someone who was very capable but without ambition...was Brother Nee....He was not ambitious at all. His work was of the highest standard. He did such a work, yet he did not keep anything for himself.

Capacity without ambition means capacity plus the cross. Everyone is ambitious. Ambition is the primary element of every fallen person's disposition. Even the lowest persons with a very low capacity are ambitious. In the church life, some are very capable and ambitious, and others are not very capable, but they also are ambitious. Yet both can cause a great deal of trouble in the church life. How marvelous it would be if everyone in the church life was against ambition. If we all could be helped to live a life against our disposition, our ambition would be killed, and there would be no problems in the church life. Once ambition is killed in the church life, the usefulness of everyone, including those of limited capacity, will come out. But when the disposition of the saints is not dealt with, ambition comes out, resulting in turmoil, the usefulness of the saints is annulled, and a great deal of devastation is brought in. (*The Experience and Growth in Life,* pp. 154, 156-157)

Matthew 16:24 says, "If anyone wants to come after Me, let him deny himself and take up his cross and follow Me." The "Me" in this verse means a great deal. This "Me" is the pattern, the pathway. Furthermore, this "Me" is the crucified and resurrected "Me." If we are not crucified and resurrected, there can be no church. The church comes into existence through the crucifixion and resurrection of Christ. Not only our self, which is defiled, but even the Lord's pure, sinless self had to be denied. If the Lord had not denied Himself and gone to the cross, He could not have been resurrected, and there would have been no church. We must follow after Him. This means that we must deny ourselves as He did and must allow ourselves to be crucified as He did. Without this, it is impossible for the church to be built up. Whenever we sense that we are feeding the self-life of another, we must say, "Lord, I will follow You. I will stop having so much contact with this brother." If you do this, the building of the church will proceed. (*The Exercise of the Kingdom for the Building of the Church,* p. 29)

Further Reading: The Exercise of the Kingdom for the Building of the Church, chs. 4-5; *The Normal Way of Fruit-bearing and Shepherding for the Building Up of the Church,* ch. 7

Enlightenment and inspiration: ______________

Morning Nourishment

Rom. 14:1 Now him who is weak in faith receive, *but* not for the purpose of passing judgment on *his* considerations.
3 He who eats, let him not despise him who does not eat; and he who does not eat, let him not judge him who eats, for God has received him.
15:7 Therefore receive one another, as Christ also received you to the glory of God.

Having a burden to care for others requires us to have a change in our disposition. Too many of us still hold on to our natural disposition. We do not contact people and invite them to our homes because they are not the same as we are....However, all nursing mothers are forced by their children to change their ways. A certain proverb says, "No mother can change her children, but all the children can change the mother." However, some...resist being changed by others in the church life. The first time the Lord met Peter and Andrew, He told them, "Come after Me, and I will make you fishers of men" (Matt. 4:19). From that time on, their business was no longer fish; it was men. After the Lord was resurrected, He came back to Peter and said, "Simon, son of John, do you love Me more than these?...Feed My lambs" (John 21:15). The Lord made the disciples fishers of men and feeders of lambs. This is to bear a burden to care for people. (*The Normal Way of Fruit-bearing and Shepherding for the Building Up of the Church,* pp. 28-29)

Today's Reading

In Song of Songs the Lord's seeker asked Him, "...Where do you pasture your flock? / Where do you make it lie down at noon?" The Lord answered, "...Go forth on the footsteps of the flock, / And pasture your young goats / By the shepherds' tents" (1:7-8). While we are seeking after the Lord, He will still remind us to follow the church and take care of the "young goats." We should not be a seeker of the Lord without any "young goats." Too many of us do not have younger ones under our care in the church life. This is a great shortcoming, and we must look to the Lord for the remedy.

According to our disposition, we like to contact people who

match our taste. However, in order to invite people and care for them, we should not have a particular taste. We must receive the believers because the Lord has received them (Rom. 14:1-3). This requires us to deal much with our natural disposition. Our disposition must be touched. This is not merely a change of our behavior; this kind of change is short-lived. Rather, we need the Lord to touch our disposition....If we mean business to love the Lord and be for His recovery, we must first have a heart for the unbelievers. We should pray, "Lord, if I cannot bring one sinner to You in one year, I simply cannot go on. Lord, I am desperate. You need to give me at least one sinner." Second, we must care for the young ones, and if there are no young ones, we can still fellowship with the other saints for mutual care. In order to have this kind of heart and burden, we desperately need our disposition to be changed.

The greatest hindrance to our usefulness is our disposition. We need to let the Lord touch our disposition, and we need to deny it. Practically speaking, to deny the self is simply to deny the disposition (Matt. 16:24). We are useless and out of function mainly due to our disposition. If we deny our disposition, we will become very useful. We may be very accustomed to our disposition and have no consciousness of it. In the church life there are many kinds of dispositions. Someone may never do anything unless the elders ask him to. He may take the excuse that he does not want to act independently, but deep in his heart he actually desires the honor of being asked by the elders. This is a shame, not an honor. In the heavenly account this may be a debit instead of a credit. Romans 14:10 says that we must give an account to the Lord at the judgment seat. The Lord will ask us to show Him the credits in our account, but when we show Him something, He may say, "No, this is a debit. You did this only to gain respect and honor." (*The Normal Way of Fruit-bearing and Shepherding for the Building Up of the Church,* pp. 29-31)

Further Reading: The Normal Way of Fruit-bearing and Shepherding for the Building Up of the Church, chs. 1-2

Enlightenment and inspiration: ______________

Morning Nourishment

1 Cor. 9:22 **To the weak I became weak that I might gain the weak. To all men I have become all things that I might by all means save some.**

John 15:5-6 **I am the vine; you are the branches. He who abides in Me and I in him, he bears much fruit; for apart from Me you can do nothing. If one does not abide in Me, he is cast out as a branch and is dried up; and they gather them and cast *them* into the fire, and they are burned.**

Our disposition is the cause for our not bearing fruit and using our talent to care for people. We are still too natural. Some persons are always slow, regardless of the situation they are in or the persons they are with. It is as if they would not even pour water on a house fire before they carefully checked what kind of water they should use. This kind of person will try to justify himself from the Bible, claiming that God is always patient and never does anything in a hurry....The Lord may be patient in every other matter, but He is quick to receive sinners. Some, though, are too quick. They bear fruit quickly, but then because they offend the fruit with their quickness, eventually they have no remaining fruit. I do not care to rebuke or expose anyone. We simply must go to the Lord and let Him shine on us. Then we will see how natural we are. By His mercy, we must have a change. (*The Normal Way of Fruit-bearing and Shepherding for the Building Up of the Church,* p. 41)

Today's Reading

In order to be useful in the Lord's hand for fruit-bearing, we must deal with our disposition. In my ministry I have seen many kinds of disposition. Some people are peculiar in their way of speaking....The more our disposition is touched, the more useful we are in the ministry of speaking for the Lord. Some were born with a disposition for speaking, but they are not genuinely useful. In order to speak for the Lord, we must be reconstituted in our being, that is, changed in our disposition.

To be an overseer requires that our disposition be dealt with in many directions. Otherwise, we are not qualified. We cannot be too slow or too quick, too strong or too soft. When there is the need to be strong, we must be strong, and when there is the need to be soft, we must be soft. Different situations require our disposition to be adjusted in different ways. An elder must truly be flexible. A good elder can speak a strong word of adjustment to a brother and then speak with him in a very pleasant way. However, this is not to play politics. We must be genuine....People are able to discern....The only way to be able to adjust a brother and then be pleasant with him is by having our disposition dealt with. The best way to be dealt with is to hate our disposition. Our disposition is the depth of our self, which must be denied. If we are not useful in the Lord's hand for taking care of people, it is due to our raw, natural disposition.

The most important thing that must be dealt with in our life with the Lord is our disposition. We must learn to have our disposition dealt with by the Lord. If we pay adequate attention to the Lord and pray much about this, it will be easy for us to care for others, bear fruit, and make a profit by using our talent. Then our entire situation will be radically changed.

Paul was this kind of person. He always spent and was spent. He meant business with the Lord. He was on earth for nothing else but to gain people. Therefore, he also said, "To the weak I became weak that I might gain the weak. To all men I have become all things that I might by all means save some" (1 Cor. 9:22). Some in the church life are too strong in their disposition to be touchable in this way; it seems that no one can cause them to be shaped. Paul, however, seemed to have no disposition of his own. He was simply like a piece of wood that could be cut into any shape. Because his disposition was fully dealt with by the Lord, it was soft, bendable, flexible, and applicable to any situation. (*The Normal Way of Fruit-bearing and Shepherding for the Building Up of the Church,* pp. 41-43, 40)

Further Reading: The Normal Way of Fruit-bearing and Shepherding for the Building Up of the Church, chs. 3, 5

Enlightenment and inspiration: ______________

____

____

____

Hymns, #840

1 Freed from self and Adam's nature,
Lord, I would be built by Thee
With the saints into Thy temple,
Where Thy glory we shall see.
From peculiar traits deliver,
From my independent ways,
That a dwelling place for Thee, Lord,
We will be thru all our days.

2 By Thy life and by its flowing
I can grow and be transformed,
With the saints coordinated,
Builded up, to Thee conformed;
Keep the order in the Body,
There to function in Thy will,
Ever serving, helping others,
All Thy purpose to fulfill.

3 In my knowledge and experience
I would not exalted be,
But submitting and accepting
Let the Body balance me;
Holding fast the Head, and growing
With His increase, in His way,
By the joints and bands supplying,
Knit together day by day.

4 By Thy Spirit daily strengthened
In the inner man with might,
I would know Thy love surpassing,
Know Thy breadth and length and height;
Ever of Thy riches taking,
Unto all Thy fulness filled,
Ever growing into manhood,
That Thy Body Thou may build.

5 In God's house and in Thy Body
Builded up I long to be,
That within this corporate vessel
All shall then Thy glory see;
That Thy Bride, the glorious city,
May appear upon the earth,
As a lampstand brightly beaming
To express to all Thy worth.

Composition for prophecy with main point and sub-points:

The Elders' Shepherding One Another, Loving One Another, and Coordinating with One Another to Be a Model of the Body Life (1)

Scripture Reading: Col. 2:19; 1 Cor. 12:31b; 13:4-8, 13; John 13:1, 14, 34; 1 Pet. 5:5

Day 1

I. In order to be a model of the Body life, the elders must know the three main principles of living in the Body of Christ:

A. The first principle of living in the Body of Christ is the relationship between the Head (Christ) and the members; the members must honor and obey the authority of the Head (Col. 2:19; 1:18a).

B. The second principle of living in the Body of Christ is the relationship between the Body (the church) and the members; the members must live in the divine fellowship to receive the life supply from the Body (1 John 1:3).

C. The third principle of living in the Body of Christ is the members' service in the Body, which is to supply life to the Body (Matt. 24:45-47; 2 Cor. 3:6).

Day 2

II. Love is the most excellent way to be an elder and a co-worker; love is not jealous, is not provoked, does not take account of evil, endures all things, never falls away, and is the greatest (1 Cor. 12:31b; 13:4-8, 13):

A. God is love (1 John 4:8); God does not want us to love with our natural love but with Him as our love; thus, we must keep ourselves in the love of God and be constrained by the love of Christ to lay down our lives on behalf of the brothers (Jude 20-21; 2 Cor. 5:14; 1 Pet. 1:22; 1 John 3:14-16; 4:7-21):

1. God first loved us in that He infused us with His love and generated within us the love with which we love Him and the brothers (vv. 19-21).

2. Not loving the brothers is evidence that one is not living by the essence and element of the divine love and is not remaining in the sphere of that love; rather, this one is living in the essence and element of the satanic death and is abiding in its sphere (3:14).
3. To abide in God is to live a life in which we love others habitually with the love that is God Himself, that He may be expressed in us (4:16).

Day 3

B. The elders should follow the pattern of the Lord in John 13 by lowering themselves to serve one another in love, humbling themselves to be a channel of supply to one another and to spiritually wash one another's feet with the water of the Holy Spirit (Titus 3:5), the holy word (Eph. 5:26), and the divine life (John 19:34) for the maintaining of their mutual fellowship in love:
   1. Through our contact with earthly things, we often become dirty; this frustrates our fellowship with the Lord and with one another.
   2. Hence, there is the need of spiritual footwashing to maintain our fellowship in love; the Lord washed His disciples' feet to show them that He loved them to the uttermost (John 13:1), and He charged them to do the same to one another in love (vv. 14, 34).
   3. We must lay aside our virtues, our attributes, our attainments, and our spirituality, humbling ourselves, emptying ourselves, and dethroning ourselves, to minister life to our fellow elders and co-workers, bringing them into intimate contact with the Lord (v. 4; 1 Pet. 5:5; Phil. 2:5-8).

Day 4 & Day 5

C. The elders need to love one another, their wives need to love one another, and they need to love one another's children (John 13:34; 1 John 4:10-11, 21; cf. Jude 12a):

1. The elders should pray for one another, have an intimate concern for one another, cherish and nourish one another, and always cover one another, speak well of one another, and never expose one another's failures and defects (2 Cor. 7:2-3; Eph. 1:15-16; Philem. 4).
2. The elders should never be critical of one another to the other saints; any issues that the elders have in their fellowship should always be kept among themselves and never told to anyone outside of their fellowship.
3. The elders should shepherd one another by shepherding one another's children; when the parents tried to bring their children to the Lord, His disciples prevented them and rebuked them, but the Lord cherished the parents by laying His hands on their children (Matt. 19:13-15; Mark 10:13-16).
4. There should be no rivalry or competition among the elders; the elders should regard one another higher than themselves, vying to show honor to one another with the Spirit, treasuring the functions of one another, and acting as one person with one mouth in one accord for the shepherding care of all the dear saints (Rom. 12:10; 15:6; Acts 2:14a).

D. The elders need to beware of ambition, pride, and unforgiven offenses:

1. Whether or not you will be useful in the Lord's hands for the long run and whether or not you will bring in the blessing for a lasting time does not depend on what you can do but on how pure your heart is; to fulfill the obligations of a co-worker or an elder, you need to have a pure heart, purified from any form of subtle ambition in intention, purpose, motive, and action in the Lord's recovery (Matt. 5:8).

2. Pride means destruction, and pride makes you a top fool; humility saves you from all kinds of destruction and invites God's grace (James 4:6; 1 Pet. 5:5).
3. In order to keep a good, excellent, and beautiful order in the church, each of the elders should not regard himself as higher, more experienced, or better than the other elders; to consider that you are superior or that you are the senior one will damage you and hurt others (Phil. 2:2-8).
4. We should never hunt to be the first in any work for the Lord (3 John 9).
5. Rivalry in the Lord's work is not only a sign of ambition but also a sign of pride (Luke 17:10; Phil. 1:15; Gal. 5:25-26).
6. To think more highly of ourselves than we ought to think is another form of pride that annuls the proper order of the Body life (Rom. 12:3).
7. Wanting to be great and not to be a servant and wanting to be the first and not to be a slave are also a sign of pride (Matt. 20:26-27).
8. The elders need to forgive one another and seek to be forgiven by one another, letting the peace of Christ arbitrate in their hearts (Col. 3:12-15).

III. The plurality of the elders in Christ's unique Body and the one accord of the co-workers in God's unique work are vital principles of the Body life:

A. "In Scripture we see that there was always more than one elder...in a local church. It is not God's will that one believer should be singled out from all the others to occupy a place of special prominence, while the others passively submit to his will. If the management of the entire church rests upon one man, how easy it is for him to become self-conceited, esteeming himself above measure and suppressing the other brethren (3 John). God has ordained that several elders together share the work of the church, so that no one individual should be able to run things according to his own pleasure, treating the church as his own special property and leaving the impress of his personality upon all its life and work. To place the responsibility in the hands of several brethren, rather than in the hands of one individual, is God's way of safeguarding His church against the evils that result from the domination of a strong personality. God has purposed that several brothers should unitedly bear responsibility in the church, so that even in controlling its affairs they have to depend one upon the other and submit one to the other. Thus, in an experimental way, they will discover the meaning of bearing the cross, and they will have opportunity to give practical expression to the truth of the Body of Christ. As they honor one another and trust one another to the leading of the Spirit, none taking the place of the Head, but each regarding the others as fellow members, the element of mutuality, which is the distinctive feature of the church, will be preserved" (*The Normal Christian Church Life,* pp. 49-50).

Day 6

B. Gideon and his three hundred men are a picture of an overcoming, blended group of co-workers, blended together into one accord to be a barley loaf, signifying the blending of the Body of Christ in resurrection for the defeat of God's enemies and for the benefit of all the people of God (Judg. 6:1-6, 11-35; 7:1-15, 19-25; 8:1-4):
   1. God gave Gideon three hundred men and made them one body, who moved and acted together in one accord, signifying the oneness in the Spirit and the living in the Body.

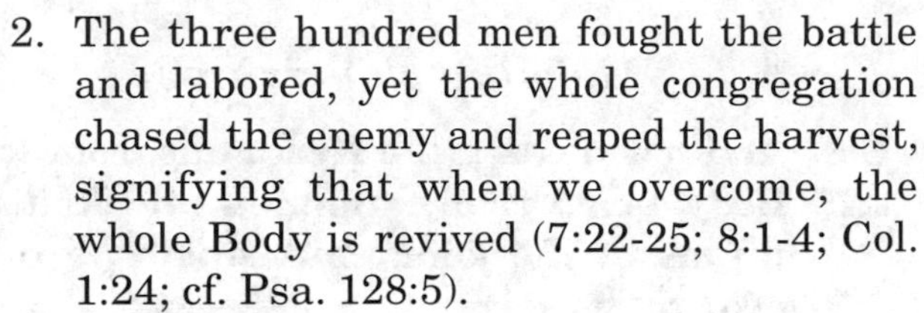

2. The three hundred men fought the battle and labored, yet the whole congregation chased the enemy and reaped the harvest, signifying that when we overcome, the whole Body is revived (7:22-25; 8:1-4; Col. 1:24; cf. Psa. 128:5).

Morning Nourishment

Col. 2:19 And not holding the Head, out from whom all the Body, being richly supplied and knit together by means of the joints and sinews, grows with the growth of God.

1 John 1:3 That which we have seen and heard we report also to you that you also may have fellowship with us, and indeed our fellowship is with the Father and with His Son Jesus Christ.

The first principle of living in the Body of Christ is to obey the authority of the Head. Both the existence of the Body and the function and activity of the Body depend on authority. Whenever authority has no place in us, the Body is paralyzed….A paralyzed body does not follow the directions of the head; where there is life, there is authority. If we want to have life, it is impossible to reject authority. Those who are full of life must obey authority….To be alive implies that we are being directed by the Head….If we have not yet been dealt with in such a way as to be rendered obedient, what we know of the Body is only a matter of theory, not of life. God must deal with our fleshly life that we may see how blessed it is to be obedient to the Head. We must aim at obedience. Many times, we seek for opportunities to make good progress, to become holy, and to become righteous. We should similarly seek for opportunities to be obedient. (*The Collected Works of Watchman Nee,* vol. 37, pp. 27-28)

Today's Reading

Our relationship with the Head is that of obedience, while our relationship with the Body is that of fellowship. Among the children of God, fellowship is a matter of reality and necessity. The life of the Body of Christ needs fellowship, without which there is only death. What is fellowship? Fellowship implies receiving of assistance from other members of the Body. For instance, I am the mouth; I can speak. But I need the fellowship of the ears in order to hear. I need the fellowship of the eyes to see. I need the fellowship of the hands to take things. I also need the fellowship of the feet to walk. Therefore, fellowship means that I receive a benefit from the special features of others.

Some Christians do not understand the principle of fellowship. They want to seek spirituality as individuals, to pray by themselves, to do everything by themselves, to be the mouth, the ears, the hands, and the feet at the same time. But those who know the Lord are not so; they need fellowship. Fellowship implies the fact that we are limited, inadequate, and willing to accept what comes from others and take it as our own.

If we see that the life of the Body is a matter of fellowship and mutual supply, we will realize that before the Lord we should not be one who consumes life but one who supplies life. If many members in the Body of Christ need the supply of life and few can afford to give the supply, the strength of the Body will fail. Therefore, we must pray for others. God will supply life to other members through this prayer. Thus, when the need in others arises, such supply will be forthcoming.

God's Word says that when one member suffers, all the members suffer [1 Cor. 12:26]; this is a fact. When one member is glorified, all the members rejoice; this is a fact....We are related in one Body....This is not only a matter of suffering or rejoicing; it is a matter of life. Some members can supply the Body with life, while others must receive life from the Body. We should have both aspects....Through fellowship we receive life from the Body, and as members we also supply life to others. When we talk of the Body, it is not a mere doctrine or teaching; the Body of Christ is an absolute fact....God's children are joined together as members of the Body. Therefore, we must gladly receive help from others, and we should also endeavor to help other brothers and sisters.

In summary, we should yield obedience to the authority of the Lord, enjoy the life of the Body, and supply life to others. These are the three main principles of our living in the Body of Christ. (*The Collected Works of Watchman Nee,* vol. 37, pp. 28-30)

Further Reading: The Collected Works of Watchman Nee, vol. 37, ch. 5

Enlightenment and inspiration: ____

Morning Nourishment

1 John 4:16 And we know and have believed the love which God has in us. God is love, and he who abides in love abides in God and God abides in him.

19 We love because He first loved us.

The end of 1 Corinthians 12 reveals that love is the most excellent way (v. 31b). How can one be an elder? Love is the most excellent way. How can one be a co-worker? Love is the most excellent way. How do we shepherd people? Love is the most excellent way. Love is the most excellent way for us to prophesy and to teach others. Love is the most excellent way for us to be anything or do anything.

Regardless of how much we shepherd and teach others, without love everything is in vain. First Corinthians 13 is a chapter covering one unique thing, that is, love. This chapter tells us that even if we prophesy in the highest way and give everything for others, without love they mean nothing (vv. 2-3). Both shepherding and teaching need love, not our natural love but His divine love. (*The Vital Groups*, pp. 74, 69)

Today's Reading

We are God's species because we have been born of Him to have His life and nature (John 1:12-13). We have been regenerated to be God's species, God's kind, and God is love. Since we become God in His life and nature, we also should be love. This means that we do not merely love others but that we are love itself. As His species we should be love because He is love. Whoever is love is God's species, God's kind.

God is love; we love because He first loved us (1 John 4:8, 19). God does not want us to love with our natural love but with Him as our love. God created man in His image (Gen. 1:26), which means that He created man according to what He is. God's image is what God is, and His attributes are what He is. According to the revelation in the holy Scriptures,

God's first attribute is love. God created man according to His attributes, the first of which is love. Although created man does not have the reality of love, there is something in his created being that wants to love others. Even fallen man has the desire to love within him. But that is just a human virtue, the very expression of the divine attribute of love. When we were regenerated, God infused us with Himself as love. We love Him because He first loved us. He initiated this love. (*The Vital Groups,* p. 69)

In 1 John 4:16 John says that he who abides in love abides in God, and God abides in him. To abide in love is to live a life that loves others habitually with the love which is God Himself so that He may be expressed in us. To abide in God is to live a life which is God Himself as our inward content and outward expression so that we may be absolutely one with Him. God abides in us to be our life inwardly and our living outwardly. Thus, He may be one with us in a practical way.

In 4:16 we see that there is an organic union between us and God. This organic union is indicated by the word "in." It is interesting that John does not say that God is love and that he who abides in God abides in love. Instead, he says that he who abides in love abides in God. To us, the former may seem more logical. But the latter is more practical and real. To say that we abide in God when we abide in love means that the very love in which we abide is God Himself. This indicates that the love that we have toward others should be God Himself. If we abide in the love which is God Himself, we then abide in God, and God abides in us.

Verse 19 says, "We love because He first loved us." God first loved us in that He has infused us with His love and generated within us the love with which we love Him and love the brothers (v. 20). (*Life-study of 1 John,* pp. 310, 312)

Further Reading: The Vital Groups, msg. 8; *Life-study of 1 John,* msg. 35

Enlightenment and inspiration: ______________________

____

____

____

Morning Nourishment

John 13:4-5 [He] rose from supper and laid aside His outer garments; and taking a towel, He girded Himself; then He poured water into the basin and began to wash the disciples' feet and to wipe *them* with the towel with which He was girded.

John 13:1 says that the Lord "loved His own who were in the world" and that "He loved them to the uttermost." Because of this love the Lord washed the disciples' feet. Hence, the foot-washing is a matter of love, a love to the uttermost. Without this, the Lord's love toward us would not have been to the uttermost but would have fallen short of our need. This shows the importance of foot-washing. This is our uttermost need. In the nine foregoing cases, the Lord has met all our needs. After all this, we still have the need of foot-washing. Therefore, the Lord has to take care of this by showing us His love to the uttermost.

The Lord washed the disciples' feet with water (v. 5). Here water signifies the Holy Spirit (Titus 3:5), the Word (Eph. 5:26; John 15:3), and the life (John 19:34)....The Lord washes us spiritually by the working of the Holy Spirit, by the enlightening of the Word, and by the operating of the inner law of life. In the Scriptures each of these three items is symbolized by water. (*Life-study of John,* pp. 328-330)

Today's Reading

Although we have the divine life and have become the church, we are still living in this fallen flesh on the earth. Through the earthly touch we are often dirtied. This is inevitable, for we cannot avoid the earthly touch. Our feet are the members of our body that touch the earth. Day by day we are touching the earth with our feet. In the ancient days of Judea, the people went almost everywhere by walking, by contacting the earth with their feet. Whenever they contacted the earth, their feet certainly became dirty. Consequently, foot-washing was a necessity for them. Spiritually speaking, it is the same for us.

Do you know when the Jews washed their feet? They washed their feet especially when they came to a feast. A feast is a center for fellowship. At that time the Jews wore sandals, and since their roads were dusty, their feet easily became dirty. If, when they came to a feast, they would have sat at the table with dirty, outstretched feet, the dirt and smell would have frustrated the fellowship. Therefore, for a pleasant feast they needed foot-washing. When the guests were invited to a feast where they fellowshipped with one another, they had to wash their feet before the fellowship. Without the washing the fellowship would have been hindered. Before they could come together to feast and fellowship at the table, they had to be washed. Otherwise, they simply could not have had pleasant fellowship.

When the Lord washed the disciples' feet, He laid aside His garments. We have seen that, in figure, garments here signify the Lord's virtues and attributes in His expression and that the laying aside of His garments signifies the putting off of what He is in His expression. If the Lord had maintained the expression of His virtues and attributes, He would have been unable to wash the feet of the disciples. Likewise, whenever you are about to wash others' feet, you need to lay aside your attainments, virtues, and attributes. This is real humility, the genuine humbling of yourself. We need to humble ourselves to such a degree that we can wash others' feet.

We must lay aside our garments, our attainments, our spirituality. We must lay aside all degrees of spirituality and become simple and general, saying to ourselves, "I am nothing, and nothing within me is special. I have only a towel, a piece of cloth, to gird me."...[We] must lay aside [our] uniforms before [we] can minister any kind of foot-washing to others. (*Life-study of John,* pp. 330-331, 338-339)

Further Reading: Life-study of John, msgs. 27-28; *Life-study of 2 Corinthians,* msg. 44

Enlightenment and inspiration: ______________

____

____

____

Morning Nourishment

Matt. 5:8 Blessed are the pure in heart, for they shall see God.

3 John 9 I wrote something to the church; but Diotrephes, who loves to be first among them, does not receive us.

To fulfill the obligations of a co-worker or an elder, you need to have a pure heart, purified from any form of subtle ambition in intention, purpose, motive, and action in the Lord's recovery. According to my over sixty years of observation, I understand the subtle words uttered by people. Some brothers who may be useful in the church behave outwardly in a humble way, but in their heart they are lifted up. That is subtle ambition, and that is a little fox that prevents them from making progress. The Lord will not give anything more to such a one, because if more is given to him, he will be lifted up. Only those who are humble without ambition can be used by the Lord, can receive gifts from the Lord, and can be entrusted with the Lord's ministry.

We should never hunt to be the first in any work for the Lord. In the church, sometimes we need to arrange for certain ones to bear certain responsibilities. Those who are not assigned may act outwardly as if they do not care, revealing nothing either in their tone or in their expression, yet inwardly they are depressed and unhappy. This is the insidious work of hidden ambition to compete with others to be the first....I want to expose the base things in our nature, such as loving or hunting to be first. May we all be enlightened to see our real condition. (*How to Be a Co-worker and an Elder and How to Fulfill Their Obligations,* p. 63)

Today's Reading

To fulfill the obligations of the co-workers and elders, first, we need to beware of ambition, and second, we need to beware of pride. Pride is an attribute of our fallen nature by birth. God has His attributes and we have ours. We are fallen human beings, and as such, the first attribute we have is pride. Who is not proud? Whoever is not proud is good for nothing. In the

Lord's work, however, we must try our best to guard against pride.

Pride means destruction. Once you become proud, your family is destroyed; once you become proud, your married life is destroyed; once you become proud, your job is destroyed. Always remember that humility saves you from all kinds of destruction and invites God's grace for you (James 4:6). God resists the proud but gives grace to the humble. If you are humble, grace comes. If you are proud, grace goes away; you have hindered grace.

This is my realization of pride. The most foolish person is a proud person, and the most wise person is a humble person. To be proud is to be a top fool.

We often are in rivalry with people in the Lord's work. For instance, a certain place began with thirty people meeting together and now they have reached one hundred thirty. Your locality began with forty people meeting together, but now you have only sixty. Because you cannot stand someone being more successful than you, a heart of rivalry arises within you. In the world, competition brings progress. In the Lord's work, however, there must not be rivalry; rivalry kills. We need to humbly say to the Lord, "O Lord, I am an unprofitable servant. Even though there are more people meeting here with me than with the other brother, I am still an unprofitable servant." In the Gospel of Luke the Lord told us that after a servant of the Lord performs many tasks during the day and comes home in the evening, he still has to say to his Master, "I am an unprofitable slave" (17:10). We all must admit that we are unprofitable servants. We should neither compare ourselves to nor compete with others. If there is an increase in the church where we serve, it is altogether the Lord's mercy. (*How to Be a Co-worker and an Elder and How to Fulfill Their Obligations,* pp. 64, 66-67)

Further Reading: How to Be a Co-worker and an Elder and How to Fulfill Their Obligations, ch. 4

Enlightenment and inspiration: ______________

____

____

____

Morning Nourishment

Rom. 12:3 For I say, through the grace given to me, to everyone who is among you, not to think more highly *of himself* than he ought to think, but to think so as to be sober-minded, as God has apportioned to each a measure of faith.

Phil. 2:3 *Doing* nothing by way of selfish ambition nor by way of vainglory, but in lowliness of mind considering one another more excellent than yourselves.

In order to keep a good, excellent, and beautiful order in the church...each of the elders should not regard himself as higher, more experienced, or better than the other elders. This is fully taught by Paul in Philippians 2. To consider that you are superior or that you are the senior one will damage you and hurt others. (*Elders' Training, Book 11: The Eldership and the God-ordained Way (3),* p. 102)

Paul told us that if we desire to live the life of the Body of Christ, we must not think more highly of ourselves than we ought to think (Rom. 12:3). Never measure yourself too highly; measuring yourself lowly is safe. To think more highly of oneself than one ought to think is another form of pride. (*How to Be a Co-worker and an Elder and How to Fulfill Their Obligations,* p. 68)

Today's Reading

Christ in His humanity humbling Himself to wash His disciples' feet (John 13:3-5) gives us a good model of how to humble ourselves for us to escape from pride....In the church, arguing about who is greater (Mark 9:34) is an ugly form of pride.

In His last journey into Jerusalem, the Lord explicitly told His disciples that He would suffer death and then be resurrected. However, the disciples were arguing about who was greater and no one cared for what the Lord said concerning His death and resurrection. The Lord taught them, saying, "Whoever wants to become great among you shall be your servant, and whoever wants to be first among you shall be your slave"

(Matt. 20:26-27). Wanting to be great and not to be a servant and wanting to be the first and not to be a slave are also a sign of pride. (*How to Be a Co-worker and an Elder and How to Fulfill Their Obligations,* p. 68)

In Scripture we see that there was always more than one elder or bishop in a local church. It is not God's will that one believer should be singled out from all the others to occupy a place of special prominence, while the others passively submit to his will. If the management of the entire church rests upon one man, how easy it is for him to become self-conceited, esteeming himself above measure and suppressing the other brethren (3 John). God has ordained that several elders together share the work of the church, so that no one individual should be able to run things according to his own pleasure, treating the church as his own special property and leaving the impress of his personality upon all its life and work. To place the responsibility in the hands of several brethren, rather than in the hands of one individual, is God's way of safeguarding His church against the evils that result from the domination of a strong personality. God has purposed that several brothers should unitedly bear responsibility in the church, so that even in controlling its affairs they have to depend one upon the other and submit one to the other. Thus, in an experimental way, they will discover the meaning of bearing the cross, and they will have opportunity to give practical expression to the truth of the Body of Christ. As they honor one another and trust one another to the leading of the Spirit, none taking the place of the Head, but each regarding the others as fellow members, the element of mutuality, which is the distinctive feature of the church, will be preserved. (Watchman Nee, *The Normal Christian Church Life,* pp. 49-50).

Further Reading: Elders' Training, Book 11: The Eldership and the God-ordained Way (3), ch. 11; *The Normal Christian Church Life,* ch. 3

Enlightenment and inspiration: ______________

____

____

____

Morning Nourishment

Acts 1:14 These all continued steadfastly with one accord in prayer, together with the women and Mary the mother of Jesus, and with His brothers.

Rom. 15:6 That with one accord you may with one mouth glorify the God and Father of our Lord Jesus Christ.

In order to take care of the church, the elders must be in one accord. Once you lose the one accord, the blessing is gone. In the New Testament, the blessing of the outpoured Spirit, which is Christ Himself (1 Cor. 15:45b; 2 Cor. 3:17), was brought in by the one hundred twenty being in one accord (Acts 1:14; 2:1-4). In the book of Acts, the one accord is mentioned five times (1:14; 2:46; 4:24; 5:12; 15:25). If we are not in one accord, we are through with the oneness of the Body, and the blessing in the church and in the work will be gone. This should be a serious warning to us. (*Elders' Training, Book 11: The Eldership and the God-ordained Way (3),* p. 102)

Today's Reading

You have to see what the landmark was of the one hundred twenty in the book of Acts. The landmark that divides the Gospels and the Acts was not the baptism in the Holy Spirit. The landmark was the one accord of the one hundred twenty. If you want to experience the baptism in the Spirit, you must have the one accord. If all the members of a local church have the one accord, the baptism in the Spirit will be there. If you really want to practice the proper way to preach the gospel, you need the one accord. Without this key, no door can be opened. The one accord is the "master key to all the rooms," the master key to every blessing in the New Testament. This is why Paul told Euodias and Syntyche that they needed this one accord (Phil. 4:2). Paul knew that these sisters loved the Lord, but that they had lost the one accord.

What we need is to recover this one accord. If we mean business to go along with the Lord's present day move, we need this one accord. Who is right does not mean anything; we need this one accord. We need to have the same mind and the same will for the same purpose with the same soul and the same heart. Philippians tells us that this matter starts from our spirit (1:27), yet we must realize we are not persons of spirit only. We are persons also of the mind, will, purpose, soul, and heart. For us to be in the same one spirit with the same one soul, one mind, and one will is to have the one accord, which is the key to all the New Testament blessings and bequests. Otherwise, we will repeat the pitiful history of Christianity by being another group of Christians repeating the same kind of disaccord. (*Elders' Training, Book 7: One Accord for the Lord's Move,* pp. 18-19)

God gave Gideon three hundred men and made them one body. Individual victory is not proper. Gideon and those three hundred men moved together and acted in one accord. All of their flesh was cut off, so they could be one. This is the oneness in the Spirit and a living in the Body. The record in the New Testament is a record of meetings rather than a record of working.

The three hundred men fought the battle, yet the whole congregation chased the enemy. The three hundred labored, yet the whole congregation reaped the harvest. When we overcome, the whole Body is revived. To stand at the bottom of the river is not for ourselves, but for the whole Body. "I...fill up on my part that which is lacking of the afflictions of Christ in my flesh for His Body, which is the church" (Col. 1:24). To be an overcomer, we also have to suffer the murmurings of the people, in the same way that Gideon suffered the murmurings of the men from Ephraim. Gideon not only defeated the Midianites from without but also defeated the Midianites from within. Only this kind of person can continue to overcome. They were "weary yet pursuing" (Judg. 8:4b). (*The Collected Works of Watchman Nee,* vol. 11, p. 774)

Further Reading: Elders' Training, Book 7: One Accord for the Lord's Move, ch. 1; *The Collected Works of Watchman Nee,* vol. 11, pp. 770-774

Enlightenment and inspiration: ____________________

____

____

____

Hymns, #913

1 Serve and work within the Body,
This the Lord doth signify;
For His purpose is the Body,
And with it we must comply.

Serve and work within the Body,
Never independently;
As the members of the Body,
Functioning relatedly.

2 As the members we've been quickened
Not as individuals free;
We must always serve together,
All related mutually.

3 Living stones, we're built together
And a house for God must be,
As the holy priesthood serving,
In a blessed harmony.

4 Thus we must be built together,
In position minister;
For the basis of our service
Is the body character.

5 In our ministry and service,
From the Body, our supply;
If detached and isolated,
Out of function we will die.

6 'Tis by serving in the Body
Riches of the Head we share;
'Tis by functioning as members
Christ's full measure we will bear.

7 To the Head fast holding ever,
That we may together grow,
From the Head supplies incoming
Thru us to the Body flow.

8 Lord, anew we give our bodies;
May we be transformed to prove
All Thy will, to know Thy Body,
And therein to serve and move.

Composition for prophecy with main point and sub-points:

The Elders' Shepherding One Another, Loving One Another, and Coordinating with One Another to Be a Model of the Body Life (2)

Scripture Reading: Acts 1:14; Ezek. 1:5-14; Judg. 5:15-16, 31

Day 1

IV. The distinction between the work of the apostles and the work of the elders is a vital principle of the Body life:

A. In God's plan He purposed that apostles should be responsible for the work in *different* places, while elders were to bear responsibility in *one* place; the characteristic of an apostle is *going;* the characteristic of an elder is *staying* (Acts 13:1-4; 16:1-4; Phil. 2:19-24).

B. Brothers such as Peter and John were elders as well as apostles (1 Pet. 5:1; 2 John 1; 3 John 1) because they were responsible not only for the work in different places but also for the church in *their own* place.

C. Only such apostles as are not traveling *much* could be elders of the church in their own locality (see *The Normal Christian Church Life,* pp. 41-46).

Day 2

V. In order to be a model of the Body life, the elders, the overseers, should meet every week for prayer and fellowship to care for the flock of God (Acts 20:28; cf. 15:6, 22):

A. This meeting is the watchtower of the whole church; we should learn to bear the breastplate every day, and then we will learn to discover something among God's people every day (Exo. 28:15-30):

1. If the church has a problem and the elders need to see how the church should go on, they should go to God with much prayer; they need to pray themselves into God, and they need to pray God into themselves.

2. In the presence of the Lord through prayer, they can read the letters on the stones of the breastplate, which is to read all the members of the church.
3. By reading the members of the church, taking the members as the letters of a divine typewriter, God's speaking will come to the elders, telling them what to do and how to do it (cf. Acts 1:14; 6:4; 13:1-4).

B. If this meeting is strong and solemn before God, all the other meetings will be spontaneously uplifted; this meeting is the center of everything.

C. No one can go home and tell his wife anything that takes place in the meeting of the overseers; in this meeting we cannot speak lightly, we cannot leak out information, and we should not have unnecessary words (Prov. 11:13; 20:18-19).

D. Unless all agree that certain matters can be made public, they should not be told to others.

E. We need to continue working until one day all the brothers and sisters respect the meeting of the overseers; they will know that this day or this half a day is the time the responsible brothers go before God to take care of things.

Day 3 & Day 4

VI. In order to be a model of the Body life, the elders must be the model and example of coordination; the elders must be coordinated, because no person is capable in everything:

A. The elders are the source of harmony in the church; if the elders are in harmony, it is impossible for the brothers and sisters not to be in harmony; disharmony in the church is fully caused by the elders (Acts 1:14).

B. When the elders are together in coordination, they are a miniature of the Body of Christ; the Lord's work is a work of the Body and by the Body for the building up of the Body; therefore, coordination is desperately needed by denying the self, taking up the cross, and losing the soul-life (Matt. 16:18-26):

1. The real coordination means that your portion is here, my portion is here, and everyone else's portion is here.
2. We may come together without much blending because everyone stays in themselves; they are afraid to offend others and make mistakes, so they keep quiet; this is the manner of man according to the flesh.
3. To be blended means that you are touched by others and that you are touching others, but you should touch others in a blending way (through the cross and by the Spirit to dispense Christ into one another for the sake of the Body).
4. Without fellowship and coordination, no one elder should speak and act independently, for to do so would annul the fact that the elders are plural in number.
5. The administration in the church is neither a democracy nor an autocracy; God's presence as resurrection is the authority (Num. 17:1-8).

C. In their fellowship with one another, the elders need to be restricted in the divine life and by the Spirit in their speaking (John 6:63; Acts 6:10):

1. Those who cover others' sins, defects, and shortcomings enjoy gain and receive blessing, but uncovering brings in a curse (Prov. 10:12; James 5:19-20; Gen. 9:21-27).
2. The elders need to realize that in their shepherding, they have to cover others' sins and not take account of others' evil (1 Cor. 13:4-7).
3. Love covers all things, not only the good things but also the bad things; whoever uncovers the defects, shortcomings, and sins of the members of the church is disqualified from the eldership (cf. Matt. 24:49).

4. The elders should not speak reviling words (to revile is to rebuke or criticize harshly or abusively; to assail with abusive language); those who take in reviling words bear the same responsibility as those who speak reviling words; in order for the church to maintain the oneness, the brothers and sisters must withstand reviling words (1 Cor. 6:10; cf. Num. 6:6; Lev. 5:3).
5. The consciousness of sin comes from knowing God; in the same way, the consciousness of reviling words comes from the knowledge of the Body; reviling words are opposed to the testimony of the Body (1 Cor. 1:10).
6. God will never entrust authority to those who by nature like to criticize others (cf. Eph. 4:29-32).
7. The elders, on the one hand, should have a clear sight over the people with much discernment, and on the other hand, they should be blind spiritually (Isa. 11:1-4a).

Day 5 **VII. Ezekiel 1 presents a beautiful picture of the coordination we need in the church life for God's expression, move, and administration (vv. 5-14):**

A. Each of the living creatures faces one direction (respectively facing north, south, east, and west), and two of their wings spread out and touch the adjacent creatures' wings, forming a square (vv. 9-12).
B. No matter in which direction the living creatures are moving, there is no need for any of them to turn; one simply goes straight forward; one returns, moving backward; and the other sides move sideways.
C. In the church service we all need to learn not only how to walk straight forward but also how to walk backward and sideways:

1. In coordination there is no freedom or convenience; coordination keeps us from making turns (cf. Eph. 3:18).
2. Before doing anything, we need to stop to fellowship and coordinate with those who serve with us.
3. Fellowship blends us, mingles us, adjusts us, tempers us, harmonizes us, limits us, protects us, supplies us, and blesses us; the Body is in the fellowship (cf. 4:4; 2 Cor. 13:14).

Day 6

D. If brothers with different functions do not know to coordinate, they will compete and even strive against each other, which could result in division (cf. Phil. 1:17; 2:2; Gal. 5:25-26):
   1. When a brother who is burdened for the gospel is functioning, moving straight forward, the brother who is burdened for shepherding should learn to walk backward; the other saints should follow these two, walking sideways.
   2. To walk backward and sideways is to say Amen to another's ministry, function, and burden (Rom. 12:4; cf. 1 Cor. 14:29-31).
   3. If we care only for our particular service and do not have these four kinds of walk, eventually we will become a problem in the church (cf. 3 John 9).
   4. The one who is walking straight forward has a prime responsibility of following the Spirit (Ezek. 1:12; cf. Acts 16:6-10).

E. We should apply this matter of coordination not only in a particular local church but also among the churches; this means that we are followers of the churches (1 Thes. 2:14).

F. The result of the coordination of the living creatures is that they become burning coals and burning torches; the more we coordinate together, the more we burn one another (Ezek. 1:13).

G. Through our coordination together in our fellowship with our precious Lord and the excellent saints, we should aspire to be the overcomers, having great resolutions in heart (making a firm decision to give our lives for the Lord's consummate recovery) and great searchings of heart (devising a great plan for the Lord's ultimate move in His recovery) (Judg. 5:15-16, 31; Dan. 11:32).

Morning Nourishment

Acts 13:1-2 **Now there were in Antioch, in the local church, prophets and teachers: Barnabas and Simeon, who was called Niger, and Lucius the Cyrenian, and Manaen, the foster brother of Herod the tetrarch, and Saul. And as they were ministering to the Lord and fasting, the Holy Spirit said, Set apart for Me now Barnabas and Saul for the work to which I have called them.**

In God's plan provision has been made for the building up of local churches, and in that plan pastors have a place, but it was never His thought that apostles should assume the role of pastors. He purposed that apostles should be responsible for the work in *different* places, while elders were to bear responsibility in *one* place. The characteristic of an apostle is *going;* the characteristic of an elder is *staying.* It is not necessary that elders resign their ordinary professions and devote themselves exclusively to their duties in connection with the church. They are simply *local* men, following their usual pursuits and at the same time bearing special responsibilities in the church. Should local affairs increase, they may devote themselves entirely to spiritual work, but the characteristic of an elder is not that he is a "full-time Christian worker." It is merely that, as a local brother, he bears responsibility in the local church. Locality determines the boundary of a church, and it is for that reason that the elders are always chosen from among the more mature believers in any place, and not transferred from other places. Thus, the local character of the churches of God is preserved, and consequently also their independent government and spiritual unity. (*The Normal Christian Church Life,* pp. 41-42)

Today's Reading

According to the usual conception of things, one would think it necessary for a considerable time to elapse between the founding of a church and the appointment of elders, but that is not according to God's pattern. The first missionary tour of the apostles covered less than two years, and during that period the apostles preached the gospel, led sinners to the Lord, formed churches, and appointed elders wherever a church had been formed. The elders were chosen on the apostles' return journey, not on their first visit to any place; but the interval between their two visits was never long, at the most a matter of months....[The apostles] appointed elders in every church....The word "elder" is relative, not absolute....Even among the spiritually immature there are bound to be those who, in comparison with the others, are more mature and have spiritual possibilities, which is all the qualification they require to be their elders.

Since Peter and John were apostles, how did it come about that they were elders of the church in Jerusalem? (1 Pet. 5:1; 2 John 1; 3 John 1). They were elders as well as apostles because they were not only responsible for the work in different places, but also for the church in *their own* place. When they went out, they ministered in the capacity of apostles, bearing the responsibility for the work in other parts. When they returned home, they performed the duties of elders, bearing the responsibility of the local church. (Only such apostles as are not traveling *much* could be elders of the church in their own locality.)...It was not on the ground of their being apostles that [Peter and John] were elders in Jerusalem; they were elders there solely on the ground of their being local men of greater spiritual maturity than their brethren.

There is no precedent in Scripture for a *visiting* apostle to settle down as elder in any church he visits; but, provided circumstances permit him to be at home frequently, he could be an elder in his own locality, on the ground of his being a local brother. If the local character of the churches of God is to be preserved, then the extra-local character of the apostles must also be preserved.

Let us note carefully that *there are no elders in the universal Church and no apostles in the local church.* (*The Collected Works of Watchman Nee,* vol. 30, pp. 42, 45-46)

Further Reading: The Collected Works of Watchman Nee, vol. 30, ch. 3

Enlightenment and inspiration: ______________________________

____

____

____

Morning Nourishment

Acts 20:28 Take heed to yourselves and to all the flock, among whom the Holy Spirit has placed you as overseers to shepherd the church of God, which He obtained through His own blood.

In every locality all the responsible brothers (those who are elders and overseers) should have an overseers' meeting every week....This is the time for the responsible brothers to pray together and to receive the brothers and sisters. This is something they must do.

This meeting is the watchtower of the whole church. The saints are not aware of many things, but you know them first. The saints have not seen many things, but you see them first. The saints have no feeling many times, but you have some feeling first. It is in this meeting that everything is sensed first. Before the difficulties around you are apparent, you can sense them in this meeting. Therefore, many times when things happen, you have anticipated the situation and taken care of it already. As time goes on, your eyes should become keener and keener. You need to learn to use your eyes to look ahead to the things in the future. (Watchman Nee, *Church Affairs,* pp. 10, 21-22)

Today's Reading

If a few responsible brothers are strong before God, their eyes will be open, they will watch and observe, and spontaneously many things will be going on with them. The high priest bore the breastplate of the twelve tribes of Israel, and he bore it all the time....He could not take it off. You should learn to bear the breastplate every day, and then you will discover something concerning God's people every day. (Watchman Nee, *Church Affairs,* p. 22)

We need to experience...reading the breastplate in the presence of God. Today we are both elders and priests. If the church has a problem and the elders need to see how the church should go on, they should go to God with much prayer. In this way the elders will become clear about what the church should do and how the church should go on. In the presence of the Lord through prayer, they can read the letters on the stones of the breastplate, which is to read all the members of the church. By reading the members of the church, taking the members as the letters of a divine typewriter, God's speaking will come to them, telling them what to do and how to do it....By this way we can have the leading from the Lord day after day concerning the church. This matter also shows how organic the eldership should be. The eldership is not organizational, but it is altogether an organic matter. The elders need to be living and exercised in contacting the Lord to be enlightened to read the situation among the Lord's people. (*Elders' Training, Book 9: The Eldership and the God-ordained Way (1),* pp. 83-84)

In the meeting of the overseers, you need to bring in all solemnity. There should not be joking and light conversation....This is the time the high priest enters into the Holiest, and this is the time we come before God to serve Him...[and] to see how the work in this area should be. Unnecessary words should be reduced, for if they abound, two or three hours will slip away and all your time will be gone. Everybody should come together in a serious way and consider things item by item.

No one can go home and tell his wife...nor can any brother go out and tell a second brother anything that happens in the meeting of the overseers. This is something divine, and everyone should maintain it....I hope that you will be strict concerning this matter....Unless all agree that certain matters can be made public, they should not be told to others. There is no need to be told every time that you cannot tell anyone. Not telling others is the principle.

If this meeting is strong before God, all the other meetings will spontaneously be uplifted. This meeting is the center of everything. If this meeting is high, all the meetings during the week will be uplifted. (Watchman Nee, *Church Affairs,* pp. 19-21)

Further Reading: Church Affairs, ch. 1; *Elders' Training, Book 9: The Eldership and the God-ordained Way (1),* ch. 6

Enlightenment and inspiration: ______________

Morning Nourishment

Rom. 12:4-5 For just as in one body we have many members, and all the members do not have the same function, so we who are many are one Body in Christ, and individually members one of another.

1 Cor. 12:27 Now you are the Body of Christ, and members individually.

The church is the Body of Christ. A local church is the expression of the Body of Christ in a locality, whereas the elders in a local church are the miniature of that expressed body. When the elders are together in coordination, they constitute the smallest form of this body, and as such they are the miniature of the Body of Christ.

In order for a church to be built up, there is first the need for the elders to be built up. How can a church be built up if its elders are not built up? The building of the church is a matter of the coordination of the saints, but if the elders within a church cannot coordinate together, how can they help the brothers and sisters to coordinate? Therefore, the building and the coordination in the church are entirely in the hands of its elders, and they are dependent upon them. Moreover, the elders must be the initiators and the examples in the building of the church. If there is no real building and coordination among the elders, there will be no initiators of the building up and the coordination of the church. In other words, there cannot be a beginning, and there is no way for the matter to be realized. Hence, for the sake of the building of the church, the elders must be the model and example of coordination. This model and example is the initiator in a local church. Only by this way can the few elders in a practical way build up and coordinate the saints together. They can do this because there is a model seen in them already. Spontaneously, they can take the saints on in this way of coordination and building. (*The Elders' Management of the Church,* pp. 113-114)

Today's Reading

Hence, we see that God's will depends on the church, and the church is fully a matter of coordination and building, while the coordination and building of the church hinges fully on the elders. The elders are the smallest miniature of the Body. If there is no coordination and building with the elders, there will be no way to talk about the coordination and building up of the church.

It is not enough for an elder to be capable on one point, in one area, or with one part only; elders have to be capable in everything. The elders must be able to think, to endeavor, to oversee, to foresee, and to achieve. They must be able to protect, to resist, and to build. There is the need for them to be all-inclusive in their ability....Yet, in many areas we have fallen short. For this reason, we have to see that the elders must be coordinated, because no one person is capable in everything.

In order to be capable in everything, there is the need for coordination. In order to have the manifold gifts, there is also the need for coordination. Many times, I am distressed about the elders in certain localities, because among them you do not see any coordination. Three or five of them may be meeting, discussing and planning there, yet among them there is no coordination. What is coordination? It means that your portion is here, my portion is here, and his portion is also here; everyone's portion is here. Yet all are in coordination. However, this is not what we see in some places. What the condition of some seems to say is that unless a certain one puts out all his portions, he will not put out anything. It is either everything or nothing. To them, it is either one person's portion, or another person's portion. If it is not your portion, then it is my portion. Either I do it all, or I do not do anything at all. This is absolutely not coordination. The real coordination means that your portion is here, my portion is here, and everyone else's portion is here. (*The Elders' Management of the Church,* pp. 114-115, 121)

Further Reading: The Elders' Management of the Church, ch. 8

Enlightenment and inspiration: ______________________

____

____

____

Morning Nourishment

Acts 1:14 These all continued steadfastly with one accord in prayer, together with the women and Mary the mother of Jesus, and with His brothers.

When all the elders are meeting together for business, none should feel that he is the responsible brother of a certain district or a certain meeting hall. The elders should only feel that they are the responsible brothers of the whole church. All the elders are the responsible ones of the church. This is why all are coordinating and fellowshipping together. When a matter is fellowshipped thoroughly enough, the feeling of God is touched, and the decision is made to do something, of course not all the elders will be involved in the work; there has to be the distribution of work. Some matters should be handled by you, while others should be handled by me. But no matter who does what, we are all doing the things together. (*The Elders' Management of the Church,* p. 122)

Today's Reading

Unfortunately, in many local churches this is not the case. When a matter is taken up by a certain elder, it becomes his responsibility. When another matter is taken up by another elder, it becomes that other elder's responsibility. When I do it, it is my job. When he does it, it has nothing to do with me anymore. Actually, there should not be feelings of this kind. When one elder speaks in one district, it should be the whole eldership speaking. When one elder makes some arrangements in one meeting hall, it should be the whole eldership making the arrangement there. This is because there is a coordination. Without fellowship and coordination, no one elder should speak and act independently....The elders are not one, but many. Whenever the elders move and speak, they do so with one another....Every report is something that represents the whole eldership, because it is something that the whole eldership has fellowshipped about and is doing in coordination. For this reason, the elders must be in coordination.

The administration in the church is neither a democracy nor an autocracy. It is not the opinion of the people, nor the proposal of one. It is fully a matter of God's presence. God's presence is the authority. In order to have the coordination, all the elders have to accept authority….Coordination in the church is neither a democracy nor an autocracy, but a body principle.

With such a coordination, the church will surely be in harmony. Disharmony in the church is fully caused by the elders. If the elders are in harmony, it is impossible for the brothers and sisters not to be in harmony. The elders are the source of harmony in the church….A church in disharmony is a punishment to the brothers and sisters. How sweet, peaceful, and happy a thing it is to have harmony in the church! (*The Elders' Management of the Church,* pp. 122-123, 130-131)

We may come together without much blending because everyone stays in themselves. They are afraid to offend others and make mistakes, so they keep quiet. This is the manner of man according to the flesh. When we come together, we should experience the terminating of the cross. Then we should learn how to follow the Spirit, how to dispense Christ, and how to say and do something for the benefit of the Body. That will change the entire atmosphere of the meeting and will temper the atmosphere. Blending is not a matter of being quiet or talkative but a matter of being tempered. We can be in harmony, because we have been tempered. Eventually, the distinctions will all be gone. Blending means to lose the distinctions. We all have to pay some price to practice the blending.

A group of elders may meet together often without being blended. To be blended means that you are touched by others and that you are touching others. But you should touch others in a blending way. Go through the cross, do things by the Spirit, and do everything to dispense Christ for His Body's sake. (*The Divine and Mystical Realm,* p. 88)

Further Reading: The Elders' Management of the Church, ch. 8; *The Divine and Mystical Realm,* ch. 6; *Messages Given During the Resumption of Watchman Nee's Ministry,* ch. 66; *Practical Talks to the Elders,* chs. 6-7

Enlightenment and inspiration: ______________

Morning Nourishment

Ezek. And from the midst of it *there came* the likeness of
1:5 four living creatures....
12 And each went straight forward; wherever the Spirit was to go, they went; they did not turn as they went.

Ezekiel 1:11b-14 reveals a very clear picture of coordination. No other verses in the Bible present the matter of coordination in such a definite and practical way.

Each of the living creatures faces one direction, respectively facing north, south, east, and west. As they face these four directions, two of their wings spread out and touch the adjacent creatures' wings, forming a square. Each of the living creatures uses two of his wings to join with other living creatures.

[In] Ezekiel 1:12...we see that every one of the living creatures goes straight forward. They do not turn, but some return, that is, move backward. For instance, while one of the living creatures is moving toward the north, the living creature facing the south must return, moving backward. Thus, one goes straight forward while the opposite creature moves backward. At the same time, the other two living creatures must move sideways. One moves sideways to the left, and the other moves sideways to the right. No matter in which direction the living creatures are moving, there is no need for any one of them to turn. One simply goes straight forward; one returns, moving backward; and the other sides move sideways. This is a beautiful picture of the coordination that we need in the church life. (*Life-study of Ezekiel,* pp. 67-69)

Today's Reading

Certain brothers and sisters cannot tolerate being coordinated together. Instead, they prefer to be separated and to do things on their own. As long as they are separated, there is no suffering. Once they are coordinated, there is a kind of suffering, because in coordination there is no freedom or convenience.

If someone acts without coordination in the church service, doing things on his own, he will make a number of turns. If he functions in the way of doing many different things by himself, it will be necessary for him to make many turns. In the church service, however, there is no need for turns. Everyone has his function and position. He can simply go straight forward in his function and position. If there is the need to move in another direction, others can take care of that. There is no need for anyone to turn.

In the church life we all need to learn not only how to walk straight forward but also how to walk backward (that is, to return) and to walk sideways. Although this may seem quite awkward, we all need to learn this lesson. Otherwise, we cannot be coordinated.

One problem is that certain brothers and sisters either want to do everything or do nothing at all. Those who want to do everything want to be able to move in every direction. If they are asked to move in a particular direction, they will also want to move in other directions. This means that they want to make a lot of turns. No matter what direction is needed in the church service, they want to be able to walk in that direction.

In the proper coordination there are no turns. You walk straight forward or you either return by walking backward or you walk sideways. It is particularly difficult to walk sideways, and many brothers and sisters are unable to do this.

We need the proper coordination in the local churches. In some churches certain brothers and sisters are very capable and make many turns. Others are not very capable, so they do nothing. As a result, there is no coordination. If we would have coordination in the church life, we all need to learn to walk straight forward, to walk backward, and to walk sideways. (*Life-study of Ezekiel,* pp. 69-70)

Further Reading: Life-study of Ezekiel, msg. 7

Enlightenment and inspiration: ______________

____

____

____

Morning Nourishment

Ezek. 1:12-13 **And each went straight forward; wherever the Spirit was to go, they went; they did not turn as they went. As for the likeness of the living creatures, their appearance was like burning coals of fire, like the appearance of torches; the fire went to and fro among the living creatures, and the fire was bright; and out of the fire went forth lightning.**

If in a local church one brother has a ministry to preach the gospel and another has a ministry to build up the saints, they must coordinate. Otherwise, they may cause a problem....The brother who is burdened for the gospel may contend for the outreach and the increase, and he may try to convince others to join him. The brother who is burdened for the building up of the saints may criticize the one who is burdened for the gospel, claiming that he brings in new ones but does not care for them. Then he might encourage others to help him to take care of the new ones. The result of this lack of coordination between these two brothers may be division, with some concerned only for the gospel and others concerned only for shepherding.

When the brother who is burdened for the gospel is functioning, moving straight forward, the brother who is burdened for shepherding should learn to walk backward. Likewise, when the brother who is burdened for shepherding is functioning and moving straight forward, the brother who is burdened to preach the gospel should walk backward. The other saints should follow these two, walking sideways, sometimes in the direction of the ministry of gospel preaching and at other times in the direction of the ministry of shepherding. (*Life-study of Ezekiel,* pp. 70-71)

Today's Reading

To walk backward is to say "Amen" to another's ministry, function, and burden. While one brother is walking straight forward according to his burden, you should say "Amen" and walk backward in coordination with him. To walk sideways is also to say "Amen" to another's function. The problem today is that in the churches there are too many turns and too little of the backward walk and the sideways walk. It is very difficult to help the brothers and sisters to walk sideways. Few are willing to walk in this way.

Ezekiel 1:12 says, "Wherever the Spirit was to go, they went." To follow the Spirit is the responsibility of the one walking straight forward; it is not the responsibility of those walking backward or sideways. If the one who is walking straight forward is not careful to follow the leading of the Spirit, the coordination will be damaged.

For example, it is right that one brother should have a ministry of preaching the gospel and that another brother should have a ministry of shepherding. But there must be the leading of the Spirit concerning the time for preaching the gospel and the time for shepherding. When it is time for the church to carry out the ministry of preaching the gospel, the brother with this ministry should take the lead under the guidance of the Spirit, and the whole church should follow and be one with this brother. Those with a different ministry or function should coordinate by walking backward or sideways.

The result of the coordination of the living creatures is that they become burning coals [v. 13]. There is a fire among them and within them. Because they are coordinated ones, God comes in as fire, and each of them becomes a burning coal.

The burning of the coals...burns out everything that is negative,...makes us fervent, intensely hot,...[and] produces the power and impact of the church. The impact in a local church comes out of the burning. This power is internal and mysterious because it comes from the burning. If you want to have impact, you must be coordinated, and in this coordination you will become burning.

From the proper coordination in a local church, there will not only be burning but also enlightening and shining. If a church is normal in its condition, it will be full of burning coals and enlightening torches [v. 13]. (*Life-study of Ezekiel,* pp. 71-75)

Further Reading: Life-study of Ezekiel, msg. 8

Enlightenment and inspiration: ______________

Hymns, #847

1 I long for fellowship in spirit,
That mingled with the saints I'll be,
Long to be saved from independence
And to be built with saints in Thee.

2 I long for fellowship in spirit,
That opened shall my spirit be,
Long to be rescued from seclusion,
And with the saints to worship Thee.

3 I long for fellowship in spirit,
Long that my spirit forth may come,
Long to be saved from self-deception,
And every hindrance overcome.

4 I long for fellowship in spirit,
With saints in spirit thus to pray,
Long for deliv'rance from pretention,
Long for true fellowship today.

5 I long for fellowship in spirit,
Long thus to know authority;
Long for true fellowship in service,
Coordinated thus to be.

6 O Lord, fulfill our heart's deep longing,
Saints for such fellowship inspire,
That we may realize Thy building
And soon fulfill Thy heart's desire.

Composition for prophecy with main point and sub-points:

Reading Schedule for the Recovery Version of the Old Testament with Footnotes

Wk.	Lord's Day	Monday	Tuesday	Wednesday	Thursday	Friday	Saturday
1	☐ Gen 1:1-5	☐ 1:6-23	☐ 1:24-31	☐ 2:1-9	☐ 2:10-25	☐ 3:1-13	☐ 3:14-24
2	☐ 4:1-26	☐ 5:1-32	☐ 6:1-22	☐ 7:1—8:3	☐ 8:4-22	☐ 9:1-29	☐ 10:1-32
3	☐ 11:1-32	☐ 12:1-20	☐ 13:1-18	☐ 14:1-24	☐ 15:1-21	☐ 16:1-16	☐ 17:1-27
4	☐ 18:1-33	☐ 19:1-38	☐ 20:1-18	☐ 21:1-34	☐ 22:1-24	☐ 23:1—24:27	☐ 24:28-67
5	☐ 25:1-34	☐ 26:1-35	☐ 27:1-46	☐ 28:1-22	☐ 29:1-35	☐ 30:1-43	☐ 31:1-55
6	☐ 32:1-32	☐ 33:1—34:31	☐ 35:1-29	☐ 36:1-43	☐ 37:1-36	☐ 38:1—39:23	☐ 40:1—41:13
7	☐ 41:14-57	☐ 42:1-38	☐ 43:1-34	☐ 44:1-34	☐ 45:1-28	☐ 46:1-34	☐ 47:1-31
8	☐ 48:1-22	☐ 49:1-15	☐ 49:16-33	☐ 50:1-26	☐ Exo 1:1-22	☐ 2:1-25	☐ 3:1-22
9	☐ 4:1-31	☐ 5:1-23	☐ 6:1-30	☐ 7:1-25	☐ 8:1-32	☐ 9:1-35	☐ 10:1-29
10	☐ 11:1-10	☐ 12:1-14	☐ 12:15-36	☐ 12:37-51	☐ 13:1-22	☐ 14:1-31	☐ 15:1-27
11	☐ 16:1-36	☐ 17:1-16	☐ 18:1-27	☐ 19:1-25	☐ 20:1-26	☐ 21:1-36	☐ 22:1-31
12	☐ 23:1-33	☐ 24:1-18	☐ 25:1-22	☐ 25:23-40	☐ 26:1-14	☐ 26:15-37	☐ 27:1-21
13	☐ 28:1-21	☐ 28:22-43	☐ 29:1-21	☐ 29:22-46	☐ 30:1-10	☐ 30:11-38	☐ 31:1-17
14	☐ 31:18—32:35	☐ 33:1-23	☐ 34:1-35	☐ 35:1-35	☐ 36:1-38	☐ 37:1-29	☐ 38:1-31
15	☐ 39:1-43	☐ 40:1-38	☐ Lev 1:1-17	☐ 2:1-16	☐ 3:1-17	☐ 4:1-35	☐ 5:1-19
16	☐ 6:1-30	☐ 7:1-38	☐ 8:1-36	☐ 9:1-24	☐ 10:1-20	☐ 11:1-47	☐ 12:1-8
17	☐ 13:1-28	☐ 13:29-59	☐ 14:1-18	☐ 14:19-32	☐ 14:33-57	☐ 15:1-33	☐ 16:1-17
18	☐ 16:18-34	☐ 17:1-16	☐ 18:1-30	☐ 19:1-37	☐ 20:1-27	☐ 21:1-24	☐ 22:1-33
19	☐ 23:1-22	☐ 23:23-44	☐ 24:1-23	☐ 25:1-23	☐ 25:24-55	☐ 26:1-24	☐ 26:25-46
20	☐ 27:1-34	☐ Num 1:1-54	☐ 2:1-34	☐ 3:1-51	☐ 4:1-49	☐ 5:1-31	☐ 6:1-27
21	☐ 7:1-41	☐ 7:42-88	☐ 7:89—8:26	☐ 9:1-23	☐ 10:1-36	☐ 11:1-35	☐ 12:1—13:33
22	☐ 14:1-45	☐ 15:1-41	☐ 16:1-50	☐ 17:1—18:7	☐ 18:8-32	☐ 19:1-22	☐ 20:1-29
23	☐ 21:1-35	☐ 22:1-41	☐ 23:1-30	☐ 24:1-25	☐ 25:1-18	☐ 26:1-65	☐ 27:1-23
24	☐ 28:1-31	☐ 29:1-40	☐ 30:1—31:24	☐ 31:25-54	☐ 32:1-42	☐ 33:1-56	☐ 34:1-29
25	☐ 35:1-34	☐ 36:1-13	☐ Deut 1:1-46	☐ 2:1-37	☐ 3:1-29	☐ 4:1-49	☐ 5:1-33
26	☐ 6:1—7:26	☐ 8:1-20	☐ 9:1-29	☐ 10:1-22	☐ 11:1-32	☐ 12:1-32	☐ 13:1—14:21

Reading Schedule for the Recovery Version of the Old Testament with Footnotes

Wk.	Lord's Day	Monday	Tuesday	Wednesday	Thursday	Friday	Saturday
27	☐ 14:22—15:23	☐ 16:1-22	☐ 17:1—18:8	☐ 18:9—19:21	☐ 20:1—21:17	☐ 21:18—22:30	☐ 23:1-25
28	☐ 24:1-22	☐ 25:1-19	☐ 26:1-19	☐ 27:1-26	☐ 28:1-68	☐ 29:1-29	☐ 30:1—31:29
29	☐ 31:30—32:52	☐ 33:1-29	☐ 34:1-12	☐ Josh 1:1-18	☐ 2:1-24	☐ 3:1-17	☐ 4:1-24
30	☐ 5:1-15	☐ 6:1-27	☐ 7:1-26	☐ 8:1-35	☐ 9:1-27	☐ 10:1-43	☐ 11:1—12:24
31	☐ 13:1-33	☐ 14:1—15:63	☐ 16:1—18:28	☐ 19:1-51	☐ 20:1—21:45	☐ 22:1-34	☐ 23:1—24:33
32	☐ Judg 1:1-36	☐ 2:1-23	☐ 3:1-31	☐ 4:1-24	☐ 5:1-31	☐ 6:1-40	☐ 7:1-25
33	☐ 8:1-35	☐ 9:1-57	☐ 10:1—11:40	☐ 12:1—13:25	☐ 14:1—15:20	☐ 16:1-31	☐ 17:1—18:31
34	☐ 19:1-30	☐ 20:1-48	☐ 21:1-25	☐ Ruth 1:1-22	☐ 2:1-23	☐ 3:1-18	☐ 4:1-22
35	☐ 1 Sam 1:1-28	☐ 2:1-36	☐ 3:1—4:22	☐ 5:1—6:21	☐ 7:1—8:22	☐ 9:1-27	☐ 10:1—11:15
36	☐ 12:1—13:23	☐ 14:1-52	☐ 15:1-35	☐ 16:1-23	☐ 17:1-58	☐ 18:1-30	☐ 19:1-24
37	☐ 20:1-42	☐ 21:1—22:23	☐ 23:1—24:22	☐ 25:1-44	☐ 26:1-25	☐ 27:1—28:25	☐ 29:1—30:31
38	☐ 31:1-13	☐ 2 Sam 1:1-27	☐ 2:1-32	☐ 3:1-39	☐ 4:1—5:25	☐ 6:1-23	☐ 7:1-29
39	☐ 8:1—9:13	☐ 10:1—11:27	☐ 12:1-31	☐ 13:1-39	☐ 14:1-33	☐ 15:1—16:23	☐ 17:1—18:33
40	☐ 19:1-43	☐ 20:1—21:22	☐ 22:1-51	☐ 23:1-39	☐ 24:1-25	☐ 1 Kings 1:1-19	☐ 1:20-53
41	☐ 2:1-46	☐ 3:1-28	☐ 4:1-34	☐ 5:1—6:38	☐ 7:1-22	☐ 7:23-51	☐ 8:1-36
42	☐ 8:37-66	☐ 9:1-28	☐ 10:1-29	☐ 11:1-43	☐ 12:1-33	☐ 13:1-34	☐ 14:1-31
43	☐ 15:1-34	☐ 16:1—17:24	☐ 18:1-46	☐ 19:1-21	☐ 20:1-43	☐ 21:1—22:53	☐ 2 Kings 1:1-18
44	☐ 2:1—3:27	☐ 4:1-44	☐ 5:1—6:33	☐ 7:1-20	☐ 8:1-29	☐ 9:1-37	☐ 10:1-36
45	☐ 11:1—12:21	☐ 13:1—14:29	☐ 15:1-38	☐ 16:1-20	☐ 17:1-41	☐ 18:1-37	☐ 19:1-37
46	☐ 20:1—21:26	☐ 22:1-20	☐ 23:1-37	☐ 24:1—25:30	☐ 1 Chron 1:1-54	☐ 2:1—3:24	☐ 4:1—5:26
47	☐ 6:1-81	☐ 7:1-40	☐ 8:1-40	☐ 9:1-44	☐ 10:1—11:47	☐ 12:1-40	☐ 13:1—14:17
48	☐ 15:1—16:43	☐ 17:1-27	☐ 18:1—19:19	☐ 20:1—21:30	☐ 22:1—23:32	☐ 24:1—25:31	☐ 26:1-32
49	☐ 27:1-34	☐ 28:1—29:30	☐ 2 Chron 1:1-17	☐ 2:1—3:17	☐ 4:1—5:14	☐ 6:1-42	☐ 7:1—8:18
50	☐ 9:1—10:19	☐ 11:1—12:16	☐ 13:1—15:19	☐ 16:1—17:19	☐ 18:1—19:11	☐ 20:1-37	☐ 21:1—22:12
51	☐ 23:1—24:27	☐ 25:1—26:23	☐ 27:1—28:27	☐ 29:1-36	☐ 30:1—31:21	☐ 32:1-33	☐ 33:1—34:33
52	☐ 35:1—36:23	☐ Ezra 1:1-11	☐ 2:1-70	☐ 3:1—4:24	☐ 5:1—6:22	☐ 7:1-28	☐ 8:1-36

Reading Schedule for the Recovery Version of the Old Testament with Footnotes

Wk.	Lord's Day	Monday	Tuesday	Wednesday	Thursday	Friday	Saturday
53	□ 9:1—10:44	□ Neh 1:1-11	□ 2:1—3:32	□ 4:1—5:19	□ 6:1-19	□ 7:1-73	□ 8:1-18
54	□ 9:1-20	□ 9:21-38	□ 10:1—11:36	□ 12:1-47	□ 13:1-31	□ Esth 1:1-22	□ 2:1—3:15
55	□ 4:1—5:14	□ 6:1—7:10	□ 8:1-17	□ 9:1—10:3	□ Job 1:1-22	□ 2:1—3:26	□ 4:1—5:27
56	□ 6:1—7:21	□ 8:1—9:35	□ 10:1—11:20	□ 12:1—13:28	□ 14:1—15:35	□ 16:1—17:16	□ 18:1—19:29
57	□ 20:1—21:34	□ 22:1—23:17	□ 24:1—25:6	□ 26:1—27:23	□ 28:1—29:25	□ 30:1—31:40	□ 32:1—33:33
58	□ 34:1—35:16	□ 36:1-33	□ 37:1-24	□ 38:1-41	□ 39:1-30	□ 40:1-24	□ 41:1-34
59	□ 42:1-17	□ Psa 1:1-6	□ 2:1—3:8	□ 4:1—6:10	□ 7:1—8:9	□ 9:1—10:18	□ 11:1—15:5
60	□ 16:1—17:15	□ 18:1-50	□ 19:1—21:13	□ 22:1-31	□ 23:1—24:10	□ 25:1—27:14	□ 28:1—30:12
61	□ 31:1—32:11	□ 33:1—34:22	□ 35:1—36:12	□ 37:1-40	□ 38:1—39:13	□ 40:1—41:13	□ 42:1—43:5
62	□ 44:1-26	□ 45:1-17	□ 46:1—48:14	□ 49:1—50:23	□ 51:1—52:9	□ 53:1—55:23	□ 56:1—58:11
63	□ 59:1—61:8	□ 62:1—64:10	□ 65:1—67:7	□ 68:1-35	□ 69:1—70:5	□ 71:1—72:20	□ 73:1—74:23
64	□ 75:1—77:20	□ 78:1-72	□ 79:1—81:16	□ 82:1—84:12	□ 85:1—87:7	□ 88:1—89:52	□ 90:1—91:16
65	□ 92:1—94:23	□ 95:1—97:12	□ 98:1—101:8	□ 102:1—103:22	□ 104:1—105:45	□ 106:1-48	□ 107:1-43
66	□ 108:1—109:31	□ 110:1—112:10	□ 113:1—115:18	□ 116:1—118:29	□ 119:1-32	□ 119:33-72	□ 119:73-120
67	□ 119:121-176	□ 120:1—124:8	□ 125:1—128:6	□ 129:1—132:18	□ 133:1—135:21	□ 136:1—138:8	□ 139:1—140:13
68	□ 141:1—144:15	□ 145:1—147:20	□ 148:1—150:6	□ Prov 1:1-33	□ 2:1—3:35	□ 4:1—5:23	□ 6:1-35
69	□ 7:1—8:36	□ 9:1—10:32	□ 11:1—12:28	□ 13:1—14:35	□ 15:1-33	□ 16:1-33	□ 17:1-28
70	□ 18:1-24	□ 19:1—20:30	□ 21:1—22:29	□ 23:1-35	□ 24:1—25:28	□ 26:1—27:27	□ 28:1—29:27
71	□ 30:1-33	□ 31:1-31	□ Eccl 1:1-18	□ 2:1—3:22	□ 4:1—5:20	□ 6:1—7:29	□ 8:1—9:18
72	□ 10:1—11:10	□ 12:1-14	□ S.S 1:1-8	□ 1:9-17	□ 2:1-17	□ 3:1-11	□ 4:1-8
73	□ 4:9-16	□ 5:1-16	□ 6:1-13	□ 7:1-13	□ 8:1-14	□ Isa 1:1-11	□ 1:12-31
74	□ 2:1-22	□ 3:1-26	□ 4:1-6	□ 5:1-30	□ 6:1-13	□ 7:1-25	□ 8:1-22
75	□ 9:1-21	□ 10:1-34	□ 11:1—12:6	□ 13:1-22	□ 14:1-14	□ 14:15-32	□ 15:1—16:14
76	□ 17:1—18:7	□ 19:1-25	□ 20:1—21:17	□ 22:1-25	□ 23:1-18	□ 24:1-23	□ 25:1-12
77	□ 26:1-:21	□ 27:1-13	□ 28:1-29	□ 29:1-24	□ 30:1-33	□ 31:1—32:20	□ 33:1-24
78	□ 34:1-17	□ 35:1-10	□ 36:1-22	□ 37:1-38	□ 38:1—39:8	□ 40:1-31	□ 41:1-29

Reading Schedule for the Recovery Version of the Old Testament with Footnotes

Wk.	Lord's Day	Monday	Tuesday	Wednesday	Thursday	Friday	Saturday
79	☐ 42:1-25	☐ 43:1-28	☐ 44:1-28	☐ 45:1-25	☐ 46:1-13	☐ 47:1-15	☐ 48:1-22
80	☐ 49:1-13	☐ 49:14-26	☐ 50:1—51:23	☐ 52:1-15	☐ 53:1-12	☐ 54:1-17	☐ 55:1-13
81	☐ 56:1-12	☐ 57:1-21	☐ 58:1-14	☐ 59:1-21	☐ 60:1-22	☐ 61:1-11	☐ 62:1-12
82	☐ 63:1-19	☐ 64:1-12	☐ 65:1-25	☐ 66:1-24	☐ Jer 1:1-19	☐ 2:1-19	☐ 2:20-37
83	☐ 3:1-25	☐ 4:1-31	☐ 5:1-31	☐ 6:1-30	☐ 7:1-34	☐ 8:1-22	☐ 9:1-26
84	☐ 10:1-25	☐ 11:1—12:17	☐ 13:1-27	☐ 14:1-22	☐ 15:1-21	☐ 16:1—17:27	☐ 18:1-23
85	☐ 19:1—20:18	☐ 21:1—22:30	☐ 23:1-40	☐ 24:1—25:38	☐ 26:1—27:22	☐ 28:1—29:32	☐ 30:1-24
86	☐ 31:1-23	☐ 31:24-40	☐ 32:1-44	☐ 33:1-26	☐ 34:1-22	☐ 35:1-19	☐ 36:1-32
87	☐ 37:1-21	☐ 38:1-28	☐ 39:1—40:16	☐ 41:1—42:22	☐ 43:1—44:30	☐ 45:1—46:28	☐ 47:1—48:16
88	☐ 48:17-47	☐ 49:1-22	☐ 49:23-39	☐ 50:1-27	☐ 50:28-46	☐ 51:1-27	☐ 51:28-64
89	☐ 52:1-34	☐ Lam 1:1-22	☐ 2:1-22	☐ 3:1-39	☐ 3:40-66	☐ 4:1-22	☐ 5:1-22
90	☐ Ezek 1:1-14	☐ 1:15-28	☐ 2:1—3:27	☐ 4:1—5:17	☐ 6:1—7:27	☐ 8:1—9:11	☐ 10:1—11:25
91	☐ 12:1—13:23	☐ 14:1—15:8	☐ 16:1-63	☐ 17:1—18:32	☐ 19:1-14	☐ 20:1-49	☐ 21:1-32
92	☐ 22:1-31	☐ 23:1-49	☐ 24:1-27	☐ 25:1—26:21	☐ 27:1-36	☐ 28:1-26	☐ 29:1—30:26
93	☐ 31:1—32:32	☐ 33:1-33	☐ 34:1-31	☐ 35:1—36:21	☐ 36:22-38	☐ 37:1-28	☐ 38:1—39:29
94	☐ 40:1-27	☐ 40:28-49	☐ 41:1-26	☐ 42:1—43:27	☐ 44:1-31	☐ 45:1-25	☐ 46:1-24
95	☐ 47:1-23	☐ 48:1-35	☐ Dan 1:1-21	☐ 2:1-30	☐ 2:31-49	☐ 3:1-30	☐ 4:1-37
96	☐ 5:1-31	☐ 6:1-28	☐ 7:1-12	☐ 7:13-28	☐ 8:1-27	☐ 9:1-27	☐ 10:1-21
97	☐ 11:1-22	☐ 11:23-45	☐ 12:1-13	☐ Hosea 1:1-11	☐ 2:1-23	☐ 3:1—4:19	☐ 5:1-15
98	☐ 6:1-11	☐ 7:1-16	☐ 8:1-14	☐ 9:1-17	☐ 10:1-15	☐ 11:1-12	☐ 12:1-14
99	☐ 13:1—14:9	☐ Joel 1:1-20	☐ 2:1-16	☐ 2:17-32	☐ 3:1-21	☐ Amos 1:1-15	☐ 2:1-16
100	☐ 3:1-15	☐ 4:1—5:27	☐ 6:1—7:17	☐ 8:1—9:15	☐ Obad 1-21	☐ Jonah 1:1-17	☐ 2:1—4:11
101	☐ Micah 1:1-16	☐ 2:1—3:12	☐ 4:1—5:15	☐ 6:1—7:20	☐ Nahum 1:1-15	☐ 2:1—3:19	☐ Hab 1:1-17
102	☐ 2:1-20	☐ 3:1-19	☐ Zeph 1:1-18	☐ 2:1-15	☐ 3:1-20	☐ Hag 1:1-15	☐ 2:1-23
103	☐ Zech 1:1-21	☐ 2:1-13	☐ 3:1-10	☐ 4:1-14	☐ 5:1—6:15	☐ 7:1—8:23	☐ 9:1-17
104	☐ 10:1—11:17	☐ 12:1—13:9	☐ 14:1-21	☐ Mal 1:1-14	☐ 2:1-17	☐ 3:1-18	☐ 4:1-6

Reading Schedule for the Recovery Version of the New Testament with Footnotes

Wk.	Lord's Day	Monday	Tuesday	Wednesday	Thursday	Friday	Saturday
1	☐ Matt 1:1-2	☐ 1:3-7	☐ 1:8-17	☐ 1:18-25	☐ 2:1-23	☐ 3:1-6	☐ 3:7-17
2	☐ 4:1-11	☐ 4:12-25	☐ 5:1-4	☐ 5:5-12	☐ 5:13-20	☐ 5:21-26	☐ 5:27-48
3	☐ 6:1-8	☐ 6:9-18	☐ 6:19-34	☐ 7:1-12	☐ 7:13-29	☐ 8:1-13	☐ 8:14-22
4	☐ 8:23-34	☐ 9:1-13	☐ 9:14-17	☐ 9:18-34	☐ 9:35—10:5	☐ 10:6-25	☐ 10:26-42
5	☐ 11:1-15	☐ 11:16-30	☐ 12:1-14	☐ 12:15-32	☐ 12:33-42	☐ 12:43—13:2	☐ 13:3-12
6	☐ 13:13-30	☐ 13:31-43	☐ 13:44-58	☐ 14:1-13	☐ 14:14-21	☐ 14:22-36	☐ 15:1-20
7	☐ 15:21-31	☐ 15:32-39	☐ 16:1-12	☐ 16:13-20	☐ 16:21-28	☐ 17:1-13	☐ 17:14-27
8	☐ 18:1-14	☐ 18:15-22	☐ 18:23-35	☐ 19:1-15	☐ 19:16-30	☐ 20:1-16	☐ 20:17-34
9	☐ 21:1-11	☐ 21:12-22	☐ 21:23-32	☐ 21:33-46	☐ 22:1-22	☐ 22:23-33	☐ 22:34-46
10	☐ 23:1-12	☐ 23:13-39	☐ 24:1-14	☐ 24:15-31	☐ 24:32-51	☐ 25:1-13	☐ 25:14-30
11	☐ 25:31-46	☐ 26:1-16	☐ 26:17-35	☐ 26:36-46	☐ 26:47-64	☐ 26:65-75	☐ 27:1-26
12	☐ 27:27-44	☐ 27:45-56	☐ 27:57—28:15	☐ 28:16-20	☐ Mark 1:1	☐ 1:2-6	☐ 1:7-13
13	☐ 1:14-28	☐ 1:29-45	☐ 2:1-12	☐ 2:13-28	☐ 3:1-19	☐ 3:20-35	☐ 4:1-25
14	☐ 4:26-41	☐ 5:1-20	☐ 5:21-43	☐ 6:1-29	☐ 6:30-56	☐ 7:1-23	☐ 7:24-37
15	☐ 8:1-26	☐ 8:27—9:1	☐ 9:2-29	☐ 9:30-50	☐ 10:1-16	☐ 10:17-34	☐ 10:35-52
16	☐ 11:1-16	☐ 11:17-33	☐ 12:1-27	☐ 12:28-44	☐ 13:1-13	☐ 13:14-37	☐ 14:1-26
17	☐ 14:27-52	☐ 14:53-72	☐ 15:1-15	☐ 15:16-47	☐ 16:1-8	☐ 16:9-20	☐ Luke 1:1-4
18	☐ 1:5-25	☐ 1:26-46	☐ 1:47-56	☐ 1:57-80	☐ 2:1-8	☐ 2:9-20	☐ 2:21-39
19	☐ 2:40-52	☐ 3:1-20	☐ 3:21-38	☐ 4:1-13	☐ 4:14-30	☐ 4:31-44	☐ 5:1-26
20	☐ 5:27—6:16	☐ 6:17-38	☐ 6:39-49	☐ 7:1-17	☐ 7:18-23	☐ 7:24-35	☐ 7:36-50
21	☐ 8:1-15	☐ 8:16-25	☐ 8:26-39	☐ 8:40-56	☐ 9:1-17	☐ 9:18-26	☐ 9:27-36
22	☐ 9:37-50	☐ 9:51-62	☐ 10:1-11	☐ 10:12-24	☐ 10:25-37	☐ 10:38-42	☐ 11:1-13
23	☐ 11:14-26	☐ 11:27-36	☐ 11:37-54	☐ 12:1-12	☐ 12:13-21	☐ 12:22-34	☐ 12:35-48
24	☐ 12:49-59	☐ 13:1-9	☐ 13:10-17	☐ 13:18-30	☐ 13:31—14:6	☐ 14:7-14	☐ 14:15-24
25	☐ 14:25-35	☐ 15:1-10	☐ 15:11-21	☐ 15:22-32	☐ 16:1-13	☐ 16:14-22	☐ 16:23-31
26	☐ 17:1-19	☐ 17:20-37	☐ 18:1-14	☐ 18:15-30	☐ 18:31-43	☐ 19:1-10	☐ 19:11-27

Reading Schedule for the Recovery Version of the New Testament with Footnotes

Wk.	Lord's Day	Monday	Tuesday	Wednesday	Thursday	Friday	Saturday
27	☐ Luke 19:28-48	☐ 20:1-19	☐ 20:20-38	☐ 20:39—21:4	☐ 21:5-27	☐ 21:28-38	☐ 22:1-20
28	☐ 22:21-38	☐ 22:39-54	☐ 22:55-71	☐ 23:1-43	☐ 23:44-56	☐ 24:1-12	☐ 24:13-35
29	☐ 24:36-53	☐ John 1:1-13	☐ 1:14-18	☐ 1:19-34	☐ 1:35-51	☐ 2:1-11	☐ 2:12-22
30	☐ 2:23—3:13	☐ 3:14-21	☐ 3:22-36	☐ 4:1-14	☐ 4:15-26	☐ 4:27-42	☐ 4:43-54
31	☐ 5:1-16	☐ 5:17-30	☐ 5:31-47	☐ 6:1-15	☐ 6:16-31	☐ 6:32-51	☐ 6:52-71
32	☐ 7:1-9	☐ 7:10-24	☐ 7:25-36	☐ 7:37-52	☐ 7:53—8:11	☐ 8:12-27	☐ 8:28-44
33	☐ 8:45-59	☐ 9:1-13	☐ 9:14-34	☐ 9:35—10:9	☐ 10:10-30	☐ 10:31—11:4	☐ 11:5-22
34	☐ 11:23-40	☐ 11:41-57	☐ 12:1-11	☐ 12:12-24	☐ 12:25-36	☐ 12:37-50	☐ 13:1-11
35	☐ 13:12-30	☐ 13:31-38	☐ 14:1-6	☐ 14:7-20	☐ 14:21-31	☐ 15:1-11	☐ 15:12-27
36	☐ 16:1-15	☐ 16:16-33	☐ 17:1-5	☐ 17:6-13	☐ 17:14-24	☐ 17:25—18:11	☐ 18:12-27
37	☐ 18:28-40	☐ 19:1-16	☐ 19:17-30	☐ 19:31-42	☐ 20:1-13	☐ 20:14-18	☐ 20:19-22
38	☐ 20:23-31	☐ 21:1-14	☐ 21:15-22	☐ 21:23-25	☐ Acts 1:1-8	☐ 1:9-14	☐ 1:15-26
39	☐ 2:1-13	☐ 2:14-21	☐ 2:22-36	☐ 2:37-41	☐ 2:42-47	☐ 3:1-18	☐ 3:19—4:22
40	☐ 4:23-37	☐ 5:1-16	☐ 5:17-32	☐ 5:33-42	☐ 6:1—7:1	☐ 7:2-29	☐ 7:30-60
41	☐ 8:1-13	☐ 8:14-25	☐ 8:26-40	☐ 9:1-19	☐ 9:20-43	☐ 10:1-16	☐ 10:17-33
42	☐ 10:34-48	☐ 11:1-18	☐ 11:19-30	☐ 12:1-25	☐ 13:1-12	☐ 13:13-43	☐ 13:44—14:5
43	☐ 14:6-28	☐ 15:1-12	☐ 15:13-34	☐ 15:35—16:5	☐ 16:6-18	☐ 16:19-40	☐ 17:1-18
44	☐ 17:19-34	☐ 18:1-17	☐ 18:18-28	☐ 19:1-20	☐ 19:21-41	☐ 20:1-12	☐ 20:13-38
45	☐ 21:1-14	☐ 21:15-26	☐ 21:27-40	☐ 22:1-21	☐ 22:22-29	☐ 22:30—23:11	☐ 23:12-15
46	☐ 23:16-30	☐ 23:31—24:21	☐ 24:22—25:5	☐ 25:6-27	☐ 26:1-13	☐ 26:14-32	☐ 27:1-26
47	☐ 27:27—28:10	☐ 28:11-22	☐ 28:23-31	☐ Rom 1:1-2	☐ 1:3-7	☐ 1:8-17	☐ 1:18-25
48	☐ 1:26—2:10	☐ 2:11-29	☐ 3:1-20	☐ 3:21-31	☐ 4:1-12	☐ 4:13-25	☐ 5:1-11
49	☐ 5:12-17	☐ 5:18—6:5	☐ 6:6-11	☐ 6:12-23	☐ 7:1-12	☐ 7:13-25	☐ 8:1-2
50	☐ 8:3-6	☐ 8:7-13	☐ 8:14-25	☐ 8:26-39	☐ 9:1-18	☐ 9:19—10:3	☐ 10:4-15
51	☐ 10:16—11:10	☐ 11:11-22	☐ 11:23-36	☐ 12:1-3	☐ 12:4-21	☐ 13:1-14	☐ 14:1-12
52	☐ 14:13-23	☐ 15:1-13	☐ 15:14-33	☐ 16:1-5	☐ 16:6-24	☐ 16:25-27	☐ 1 Cor 1:1-4

Reading Schedule for the Recovery Version of the New Testament with Footnotes

Wk.	Lord's Day	Monday	Tuesday	Wednesday	Thursday	Friday	Saturday
53	☐ 1 Cor 1:5-9	☐ 1:10-17	☐ 1:18-31	☐ 2:1-5	☐ 2:6-10	☐ 2:11-16	☐ 3:1-9
54	☐ 3:10-13	☐ 3:14-23	☐ 4:1-9	☐ 4:10-21	☐ 5:1-13	☐ 6:1-11	☐ 6:12-20
55	☐ 7:1-16	☐ 7:17-24	☐ 7:25-40	☐ 8:1-13	☐ 9:1-15	☐ 9:16-27	☐ 10:1-4
56	☐ 10:5-13	☐ 10:14-33	☐ 11:1-6	☐ 11:7-16	☐ 11:17-26	☐ 11:27-34	☐ 12:1-11
57	☐ 12:12-22	☐ 12:23-31	☐ 13:1-13	☐ 14:1-12	☐ 14:13-25	☐ 14:26-33	☐ 14:34-40
58	☐ 15:1-19	☐ 15:20-28	☐ 15:29-34	☐ 15:35-49	☐ 15:50-58	☐ 16:1-9	☐ 16:10-24
59	☐ 2 Cor 1:1-4	☐ 1:5-14	☐ 1:15-22	☐ 1:23—2:11	☐ 2:12-17	☐ 3:1-6	☐ 3:7-11
60	☐ 3:12-18	☐ 4:1-6	☐ 4:7-12	☐ 4:13-18	☐ 5:1-8	☐ 5:9-15	☐ 5:16-21
61	☐ 6:1-13	☐ 6:14—7:4	☐ 7:5-16	☐ 8:1-15	☐ 8:16-24	☐ 9:1-15	☐ 10:1-6
62	☐ 10:7-18	☐ 11:1-15	☐ 11:16-33	☐ 12:1-10	☐ 12:11-21	☐ 13:1-10	☐ 13:11-14
63	☐ Gal 1:1-5	☐ 1:6-14	☐ 1:15-24	☐ 2:1-13	☐ 2:14-21	☐ 3:1-4	☐ 3:5-14
64	☐ 3:15-22	☐ 3:23-29	☐ 4:1-7	☐ 4:8-20	☐ 4:21-31	☐ 5:1-12	☐ 5:13-21
65	☐ 5:22-26	☐ 6:1-10	☐ 6:11-15	☐ 6:16-18	☐ Eph 1:1-3	☐ 1:4-6	☐ 1:7-10
66	☐ 1:11-14	☐ 1:15-18	☐ 1:19-23	☐ 2:1-5	☐ 2:6-10	☐ 2:11-14	☐ 2:15-18
67	☐ 2:19-22	☐ 3:1-7	☐ 3:8-13	☐ 3:14-18	☐ 3:19-21	☐ 4:1-4	☐ 4:5-10
68	☐ 4:11-16	☐ 4:17-24	☐ 4:25-32	☐ 5:1-10	☐ 5:11-21	☐ 5:22-26	☐ 5:27-33
69	☐ 6:1-9	☐ 6:10-14	☐ 6:15-18	☐ 6:19-24	☐ Phil 1:1-7	☐ 1:8-18	☐ 1:19-26
70	☐ 1:27—2:4	☐ 2:5-11	☐ 2:12-16	☐ 2:17-30	☐ 3:1-6`	☐ 3:7-11	☐ 3:12-16
71	☐ 3:17-21	☐ 4:1-9	☐ 4:10-23	☐ Col 1:1-8	☐ 1:9-13	☐ 1:14-23	☐ 1:24-29
72	☐ 2:1-7	☐ 2:8-15	☐ 2:16-23	☐ 3:1-4	☐ 3:5-15	☐ 3:16-25	☐ 4:1-18
73	☐ 1 Thes 1:1-3	☐ 1:4-10	☐ 2:1-12	☐ 2:13—3:5	☐ 3:6-13	☐ 4:1-10	☐ 4:11—5:11
74	☐ 5:12-28	☐ 2 Thes 1:1-12	☐ 2:1-17	☐ 3:1-18	☐ 1 Tim 1:1-2	☐ 1:3-4	☐ 1:5-14
75	☐ 1:15-20	☐ 2:1-7	☐ 2:8-15	☐ 3:1-13	☐ 3:14—4:5	☐ 4:6-16	☐ 5:1-25
76	☐ 6:1-10	☐ 6:11-21	☐ 2 Tim 1:1-10	☐ 1:11-18	☐ 2:1-15	☐ 2:16-26	☐ 3:1-13
77	☐ 3:14—4:8	☐ 4:9-22	☐ Titus 1:1-4	☐ 1:5-16	☐ 2:1-15	☐ 3:1-8	☐ 3:9-15
78	☐ Philem 1:1-11	☐ 1:12-25	☐ Heb 1:1-2	☐ 1:3-5	☐ 1:6-14	☐ 2:1-9	☐ 2:10-18

Reading Schedule for the Recovery Version of the New Testament with Footnotes

Wk.	Lord's Day	Monday	Tuesday	Wednesday	Thursday	Friday	Saturday
79	☐ Heb 3:1-6	☐ 3:7-19	☐ 4:1-9	☐ 4:10-13	☐ 4:14-16	☐ 5:1-10	☐ 5:11—6:3
80	☐ 6:4-8	☐ 6:9-20	☐ 7:1-10	☐ 7:11-28	☐ 8:1-6	☐ 8:7-13	☐ 9:1-4
81	☐ 9:5-14	☐ 9:15-28	☐ 10:1-18	☐ 10:19-28	☐ 10:29-39	☐ 11:1-6	☐ 11:7-19
82	☐ 11:20-31	☐ 11:32-40	☐ 12:1-2	☐ 12:3-13	☐ 12:14-17	☐ 12:18-26	☐ 12:27-29
83	☐ 13:1-7	☐ 13:8-12	☐ 13:13-15	☐ 13:16-25	☐ James 1:1-8	☐ 1:9-18	☐ 1:19-27
84	☐ 2:1-13	☐ 2:14-26	☐ 3:1-18	☐ 4:1-10	☐ 4:11-17	☐ 5:1-12	☐ 5:13-20
85	☐ 1 Pet 1:1-2	☐ 1:3-4	☐ 1:5	☐ 1:6-9	☐ 1:10-12	☐ 1:13-17	☐ 1:18-25
86	☐ 2:1-3	☐ 2:4-8	☐ 2:9-17	☐ 2:18-25	☐ 3:1-13	☐ 3:14-22	☐ 4:1-6
87	☐ 4:7-16	☐ 4:17-19	☐ 5:1-4	☐ 5:5-9	☐ 5:10-14	☐ 2 Pet 1:1-2	☐ 1:3-4
88	☐ 1:5-8	☐ 1:9-11	☐ 1:12-18	☐ 1:19-21	☐ 2:1-3	☐ 2:4-11	☐ 2:12-22
89	☐ 3:1-6	☐ 3:7-9	☐ 3:10-12	☐ 3:13-15	☐ 3:16	☐ 3:17-18	☐ 1 John 1:1-2
90	☐ 1:3-4	☐ 1:5	☐ 1:6	☐ 1:7	☐ 1:8-10	☐ 2:1-2	☐ 2:3-11
91	☐ 2:12-14	☐ 2:15-19	☐ 2:20-23	☐ 2:24-27	☐ 2:28-29	☐ 3:1-5	☐ 3:6-10
92	☐ 3:11-18	☐ 3:19-24	☐ 4:1-6	☐ 4:7-11	☐ 4:12-15	☐ 4:16—5:3	☐ 5:4-13
93	☐ 5:14-17	☐ 5:18-21	☐ 2 John 1:1-3	☐ 1:4-9	☐ 1:10-13	☐ 3 John 1:1-6	☐ 1:7-14
94	☐ Jude 1:1-4	☐ 1:5-10	☐ 1:11-19	☐ 1:20-25	☐ Rev 1:1-3	☐ 1:4-6	☐ 1:7-11
95	☐ 1:12-13	☐ 1:14-16	☐ 1:17-20	☐ 2:1-6	☐ 2:7	☐ 2:8-9	☐ 2:10-11
96	☐ 2:12-14	☐ 2:15-17	☐ 2:18-23	☐ 2:24-29	☐ 3:1-3	☐ 3:4-6	☐ 3:7-9
97	☐ 3:10-13	☐ 3:14-18	☐ 3:19-22	☐ 4:1-5	☐ 4:6-7	☐ 4:8-11	☐ 5:1-6
98	☐ 5:7-14	☐ 6:1-8	☐ 6:9-17	☐ 7:1-8	☐ 7:9-17	☐ 8:1-6	☐ 8:7-12
99	☐ 8:13—9:11	☐ 9:12-21	☐ 10:1-4	☐ 10:5-11	☐ 11:1-4	☐ 11:5-14	☐ 11:15-19
100	☐ 12:1-4	☐ 12:5-9	☐ 12:10-18	☐ 13:1-10	☐ 13:11-18	☐ 14:1-5	☐ 14:6-12
101	☐ 14:13-20	☐ 15:1-8	☐ 16:1-12	☐ 16:13-21	☐ 17:1-6	☐ 17:7-18	☐ 18:1-8
102	☐ 18:9—19:4	☐ 19:5-10	☐ 19:11-16	☐ 19:17-21	☐ 20:1-6	☐ 20:7-10	☐ 20:11-15
103	☐ 21:1	☐ 21:2	☐ 21:3-8	☐ 21:9-13	☐ 21:14-18	☐ 21:19-21	☐ 21:22-27
104	☐ 22:1	☐ 22:2	☐ 22:3-11	☐ 22:12-15	☐ 22:16-17	☐ 22:18-21	☐

Week 1 — Day 4 **Today's verses**

John I am the vine; you are the branches. He
15:5 who abides in Me and I in him, he bears
much fruit; for apart from Me you can do
nothing.

Date

Week 1 — Day 5 **Today's verses**

2 Cor. Who has also made us sufficient as minis-
3:6 ters of a new covenant, *ministers* not of
the letter but of the Spirit; for the letter
kills, but the Spirit gives life.
7:13 Because of this we have been comforted.
And in addition to our comfort, we rejoiced more abundantly over the joy of Titus, because his spirit has been refreshed
by all of you.

Date

Week 1 — Day 6 **Today's verses**

1 Cor. ...And moreover I show to you a most ex-
12:31 cellent way.
13:7 [Love] covers all things, believes all
things, hopes all things, endures all
things.

Date

Week 1 — Day 1 **Today's verses**

John Then when they had eaten breakfast, Jesus
21:15-17 said to Simon Peter, Simon, *son* of John, do
you love Me more than these? He said to
Him, Yes, Lord, You know that I love You.
He said to him, Feed My lambs. He said to
him again a second time, Simon, *son* of
John, do you love Me? He said to Him, Yes,
Lord, You know that I love You. He said to
him, Shepherd My sheep. He said to him
the third time, Simon, *son* of John, do you
love Me? Peter was grieved that He said to
him the third time, Do you love Me? And he
said to Him, Lord, You know all things; You
know that I love You. Jesus said to him, Feed
My sheep.

Date

Week 1 — Day 2 **Today's verses**

Matt. And as He was reclining *at table* in the
9:10 house, behold, many tax collectors and
sinners came and reclined together with
Jesus and His disciples.
Luke The Son of Man has come eating and
7:34 drinking, and you say, Behold, a gluttonous man and a drunkard, a friend of tax
collectors and sinners.
Matt. Who then is the faithful and prudent
24:45 slave, whom the master has set over his
household to give them food at the proper
time?

Date

Week 1 — Day 3 **Today's verses**

John He said to him the third time, Simon, *son*
21:17 of John, do you love Me? Peter was
grieved that He said to him the third time,
Do you love Me? And he said to Him,
Lord, You know all things; You know that I
love You. Jesus said to him, Feed My
sheep.

Date

Week 2 — Day 4 **Today's verses**

Acts Serving the Lord as a slave with all humil-
20:19-20 ity and tears and trials which came upon
me by the plots of the Jews; how I did not
withhold any of those things that are profitable by not declaring *them* to you and by
not teaching you publicly and from house
to house.
27 For I did not shrink from declaring to you
all the counsel of God.

Date

Week 2 — Day 5 **Today's verses**

Acts And now, behold, I am going bound in
20:22 the spirit to Jerusalem, not knowing what
will meet me there.
2 Cor. I entreated Titus and sent with *him* the
12:18-19 brother. Titus did not take advantage of
you, did he? Did we not walk in the same
spirit? In the same steps? All this time you
have been thinking that we are defending
ourselves to you. Before God in Christ we
speak; but all things, beloved, *are* for your
building up.

Date

Week 2 — Day 6 **Today's verses**

Acts Therefore watch, remembering that for
20:31-34 three years, night and day, I did not cease
admonishing each one with tears. And
now I commit you to God and to the word
of His grace, which is able to build *you* up
and to give *you* the inheritance among all
those who have been sanctified. I have
coveted no one's silver or gold or clothing. You yourselves know that these
hands have ministered to my needs and to
those who are with me.

Date

Week 2 — Day 1 **Today's verses**

Matt. A good tree cannot produce bad fruit, nei-
7:18 ther can a corrupt tree produce good fruit.
2 Tim. But in a great house there are not only
2:20-21 gold and silver vessels but also wooden
and earthen; and some are unto honor,
and some unto dishonor. If therefore anyone cleanses himself from these, he will
be a vessel unto honor, sanctified, useful
to the master, prepared unto every good
work.

Date

Week 2 — Day 2 **Today's verses**

Phil. Be imitators together of me, brothers, and
3:17 observe those who thus walk even as you
have us as a pattern.
1 Tim. …That in me, the foremost, Jesus Christ
1:16 might display all His long-suffering for a
pattern to those who are to believe on
Him unto eternal life.
4:12 Let no one despise your youth, but be a
pattern to the believers in word, in conduct, in love, in faith, in purity.
1 Pet. Nor as lording it over your allotments but
5:3 by becoming patterns of the flock.

Date

Week 2 — Day 3 **Today's verses**

Acts …You yourselves know, from the first day
20:18 that I set foot in Asia, how I was with you
all the time.
28 Take heed to yourselves and to all the
flock, among whom the Holy Spirit has
placed you as overseers to shepherd the
church of God, which He obtained
through His own blood.
35 In all things I have shown you by example
that toiling in this way we ought to support the weak and to remember the words
of the Lord Jesus, that He Himself said, It
is more blessed to give than to receive.

Date

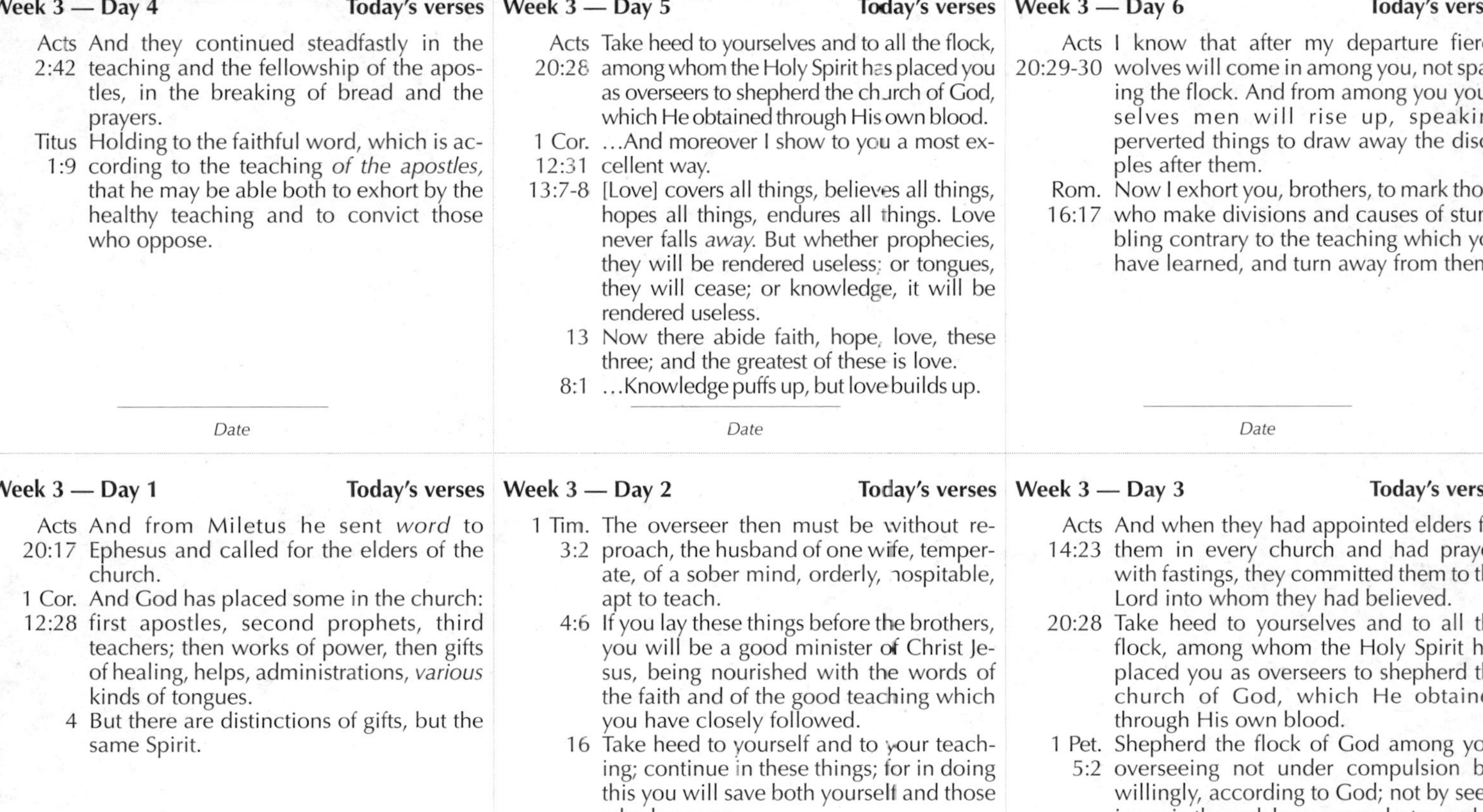

Week 3 — Day 4 **Today's verses**

Acts And they continued steadfastly in the
2:42 teaching and the fellowship of the apostles, in the breaking of bread and the prayers.
Titus Holding to the faithful word, which is ac-
1:9 cording to the teaching *of the apostles,* that he may be able both to exhort by the healthy teaching and to convict those who oppose.

Date

Week 3 — Day 5 **Today's verses**

Acts Take heed to yourselves and to all the flock,
20:28 among whom the Holy Spirit has placed you as overseers to shepherd the church of God, which He obtained through His own blood.
1 Cor. ...And moreover I show to you a most ex-
12:31 cellent way.
13:7-8 [Love] covers all things, believes all things, hopes all things, endures all things. Love never falls *away.* But whether prophecies, they will be rendered useless; or tongues, they will cease; or knowledge, it will be rendered useless.
13 Now there abide faith, hope, love, these three; and the greatest of these is love.
8:1 ...Knowledge puffs up, but love builds up.

Date

Week 3 — Day 6 **Today's verses**

Acts I know that after my departure fierce
20:29-30 wolves will come in among you, not sparing the flock. And from among you yourselves men will rise up, speaking perverted things to draw away the disciples after them.
Rom. Now I exhort you, brothers, to mark those
16:17 who make divisions and causes of stumbling contrary to the teaching which you have learned, and turn away from them.

Date

Week 3 — Day 1 **Today's verses**

Acts And from Miletus he sent *word* to
20:17 Ephesus and called for the elders of the church.
1 Cor. And God has placed some in the church:
12:28 first apostles, second prophets, third teachers; then works of power, then gifts of healing, helps, administrations, *various* kinds of tongues.
4 But there are distinctions of gifts, but the same Spirit.

Date

Week 3 — Day 2 **Today's verses**

1 Tim. The overseer then must be without re-
3:2 proach, the husband of one wife, temperate, of a sober mind, orderly, hospitable, apt to teach.
4:6 If you lay these things before the brothers, you will be a good minister of Christ Jesus, being nourished with the words of the faith and of the good teaching which you have closely followed.
16 Take heed to yourself and to your teaching; continue in these things; for in doing this you will save both yourself and those who hear you.

Date

Week 3 — Day 3 **Today's verses**

Acts And when they had appointed elders for
14:23 them in every church and had prayed with fastings, they committed them to the Lord into whom they had believed.
20:28 Take heed to yourselves and to all the flock, among whom the Holy Spirit has placed you as overseers to shepherd the church of God, which He obtained through His own blood.
1 Pet. Shepherd the flock of God among you,
5:2 overseeing not under compulsion but willingly, according to God; not by seeking gain through base means but eagerly.

Date

Week 4 — Day 4 **Today's verses**

Matt. 19:5-6 And [He] said, "For this cause shall a man leave his father and his mother and shall be joined to his wife; and the two shall be one flesh"?...Therefore what God has yoked together, let man not separate.

Date

Week 4 — Day 5 **Today's verses**

Exo. 21:5-6 But if the servant plainly says, I love my master, my wife, and my children; I will not go out free; then his master shall bring him to God and shall bring him to the door or to the doorpost, and his master shall bore his ear through with an awl; and he shall serve him forever.

Date

Week 4 — Day 6 **Today's verses**

Col. 1:28 Whom we announce, admonishing every man and teaching every man in all wisdom that we may present every man full-grown in Christ.

Lev. 10:17 ...For [the sin offering] is most holy, and He gave it to you to bear the iniquity of the assembly, to make expiation for them before Jehovah.

Date

Week 4 — Day 1 **Today's verses**

Heb. 13:17 Obey the ones leading you and submit to *them,* for they watch over your souls as those who will render an account, that they may do this with joy and not groaning; for this would be unprofitable to you.

1 Pet. 5:2 Shepherd the flock of God among you, overseeing not under compulsion but willingly, according to God; not by seeking gain through base means but eagerly.

Date

Week 4 — Day 2 **Today's verses**

Luke 10:2 ...He said to them, The harvest is great, but the workers few; therefore, beseech the Lord of the harvest that He would thrust out workers into His harvest.

Acts 15:28 For it seemed good to the Holy Spirit and to us...

Date

Week 4 — Day 3 **Today's verses**

Acts 13:2-4 And as they were ministering to the Lord and fasting, the Holy Spirit said, Set apart for Me now Barnabas and Saul for the work to which I have called them. Then, when they had fasted and prayed and laid their hands on them, they sent them away. They then, having been sent out by the Holy Spirit...

Date

Week 5 — Day 4 **Today's verses**

2 Cor. Our mouth is opened to you, Corinthians;
6:11-13 our heart is enlarged. You are not constricted in us, but you are constricted in your inward parts. But for a recompense in kind, I speak as to children, you also be enlarged.

Date

Week 5 — Day 5 **Today's verses**

1 Kings Give therefore to Your servant an under-
3:9-10 standing heart to judge Your people and to discern between good and evil. For who is able to judge this great people of Yours? And this word seemed good in the sight of the Lord, that Solomon had asked for this matter.
4:29 And God gave Solomon wisdom and very much understanding and largeness of heart, even as the sand that is on the seashore.

Date

Week 5 — Day 6 **Today's verses**

2 Cor. Make room for us; we have wronged no
7:2-3 one, we have corrupted no one, we have taken advantage of no one. I do not say *this* to condemn *you,* for I have said before that you are in our hearts for *our* dying together and *our* living together.
8:1 Furthermore we make known to you, brothers, the grace of God which has been given in the churches of Macedonia.
4 With much entreaty they besought of us the grace and the fellowship of the ministry to the saints.

Date

Week 5 — Day 1 **Today's verses**

2 Cor. For the love of Christ constrains us be-
5:14-15 cause we have judged this, that One died for all, therefore all died; and He died for all that those who live may no longer live to themselves but to Him who died for them and has been raised.
18 But all things are out from God, who has reconciled us to Himself through Christ and has given to us the ministry of reconciliation.
21 Him who did not know sin He made sin on our behalf that we might become the righteousness of God in Him.

Date

Week 5 — Day 2 **Today's verses**

2 Cor. But all things are out from God, who has
5:18-20 reconciled us to Himself through Christ and has given to us the ministry of reconciliation; namely, that God in Christ was reconciling the world to Himself, not accounting their offenses to them, and has put in us the word of reconciliation. On behalf of Christ then we are ambassadors, as God entreats *you* through us; we beseech *you* on behalf of Christ, Be reconciled to God.

Date

Week 5 — Day 3 **Today's verses**

2 Cor. On behalf of Christ then we are ambassa-
5:20 dors, as God entreats *you* through us; we beseech *you* on behalf of Christ, Be reconciled to God.
6:1-2 And working together with *Him,* we also entreat you not to receive the grace of God in vain; for He says, "In an acceptable time I listened to you, and in the day of salvation I helped you." Behold, now is the well-acceptable time; behold, now is the day of salvation.

Date

Week 6 — Day 4 **Today's verses**

Rom. Knowing this, that our old man has been
6:6 crucified with *Him*...
Gal. I am crucified with Christ; and *it is* no lon-
2:20 ger I *who* live, but *it is* Christ *who* lives in me;
and the *life* which I now live in the flesh I live
in faith, the *faith* of the Son of God, who loved
me and gave Himself up for me.

Date

Week 6 — Day 5 **Today's verses**

Rom. Now him who is weak in faith receive,
14:1 *but* not for the purpose of passing judgment on *his* considerations.
3 He who eats, let him not despise him who
does not eat; and he who does not eat, let
him not judge him who eats, for God has
received him.
15:7 Therefore receive one another, as Christ
also received you to the glory of God.

Date

Week 6 — Day 6 **Today's verses**

1 Cor. To the weak I became weak that I might
9:22 gain the weak. To all men I have become
all things that I might by all means save
some.
John I am the vine; you are the branches. He
15:5-6 who abides in Me and I in him, he bears
much fruit; for apart from Me you can do
nothing. If one does not abide in Me, he is
cast out as a branch and is dried up; and
they gather them and cast *them* into the
fire, and they are burned.

Date

Week 6 — Day 1 **Today's verses**

2 Pet. And for this very reason also, adding all
1:5-8 diligence, supply bountifully in your faith
virtue; and in virtue, knowledge; and in
knowledge, self-control; and in self-control, endurance; and in endurance, godliness; and in godliness, brotherly love; and
in brotherly love, love. For these things,
existing in you and abounding, constitute
you neither idle nor unfruitful unto the
full knowledge of our Lord Jesus Christ.

Date

Week 6 — Day 2 **Today's verses**

Matt. Then Jesus said,...If anyone wants to
16:24-26 come after Me, let him deny himself and
take up his cross and follow Me. For whoever wants to save his soul-life shall lose
it; but whoever loses his soul-life for My
sake shall find it. For what shall a man be
profited if he gains the whole world, but
forfeits his soul-life? Or what shall a man
give in exchange for his soul-life?

Date

Week 6 — Day 3 **Today's verses**

Luke ...If anyone wants to come after Me, let
9:23 him deny himself and take up his cross
daily and follow Me.
Matt. And when the disciples heard *this,* they
19:25-26 were greatly astonished and said, Who
then can be saved? And looking upon
them, Jesus said to them, With men this is
impossible, but with God all things are
possible.

Date

Week 7 — Day 4 **Today's verses**

Matt. Blessed are the pure in heart, for they
5:8 shall see God.
3 John I wrote something to the church; but
9 Diotrephes, who loves to be first among
them, does not receive us.

Date

Week 7 — Day 5 **Today's verses**

Rom. For I say, through the grace given to me, to
12:3 everyone who is among you, not to think
more highly *of himself* than he ought to
think, but to think so as to be sober-minded, as God has apportioned to
each a measure of faith.
Phil. Doing nothing by way of selfish ambition
2:3 nor by way of vainglory, but in lowliness
of mind considering one another more
excellent than yourselves.

Date

Week 7 — Day 6 **Today's verses**

Acts These all continued steadfastly with one
1:14 accord in prayer, together with the
women and Mary the mother of Jesus,
and with His brothers.
Rom. That with one accord you may with one
15:6 mouth glorify the God and Father of our
Lord Jesus Christ.

Date

Week 7 — Day 1 **Today's verses**

Col. And not holding the Head, out from
2:19 whom all the Body, being richly supplied
and knit together by means of the joints
and sinews, grows with the growth of
God.
1 John That which we have seen and heard we
1:3 report also to you that you also may have
fellowship with us, and indeed our fellowship is with the Father and with His
Son Jesus Christ.

Date

Week 7 — Day 2 **Today's verses**

1 John And we know and have believed the love
4:16 which God has in us. God is love, and he
who abides in love abides in God and
God abides in him.
19 We love because He first loved us.

Date

Week 7 — Day 3 **Today's verses**

John [He] rose from supper and laid aside His
13:4-5 outer garments; and taking a towel, He
girded Himself; then He poured water
into the basin and began to wash the disciples' feet and to wipe *them* with the
towel with which He was girded.

Date

Week 8 — Day 4 **Today's verses**

Acts 1:14 These all continued steadfastly with one accord in prayer, together with the women and Mary the mother of Jesus, and with His brothers.

Date

Week 8 — Day 5 **Today's verses**

Ezek. 1:5 And from the midst of it *there came* the likeness of four living creatures....
12 And each went straight forward; wherever the Spirit was to go, they went; they did not turn as they went.

Date

Week 8 — Day 5 **Today's verses**

Ezek. 1:12-13 And each went straight forward; wherever the Spirit was to go, they went; they did not turn as they went. As for the likeness of the living creatures, their appearance was like burning coals of fire, like the appearance of torches; the fire went to and fro among the living creatures, and the fire was bright; and out of the fire went forth lightning.

Date

Week 8 — Day 1 **Today's verses**

Acts 13:1-2 Now there were in Antioch, in the local church, prophets and teachers: Barnabas and Simeon, who was called Niger, and Lucius the Cyrenian, and Manaen, the foster brother of Herod the tetrarch, and Saul. And as they were ministering to the Lord and fasting, the Holy Spirit said, Set apart for Me now Barnabas and Saul for the work to which I have called them.

Date

Week 8 — Day 2 **Today's verses**

Acts 20:28 Take heed to yourselves and to all the flock, among whom the Holy Spirit has placed you as overseers to shepherd the church of God, which He obtained through His own blood.

Date

Week 8 — Day 3 **Today's verses**

Rom. 12:4-5 For just as in one body we have many members, and all the members do not have the same function, so we who are many are one Body in Christ, and individually members one of another.

1 Cor. 12:27 Now you are the Body of Christ, and members individually.

Date